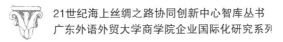

21世纪海上丝绸之路协同创新中心智库丛书

广东外语外贸大学商学院企业国际化研究系列

U0620563

新时期中国商业银行 CSR建设研究

朱文忠　王敏　刘世平　程霞◎著

THE CONSTRUCTION OF CHINESE COMMERCIAL BANKS' CSR VALUE IN THE NEW ERA

经济管理出版社

ECONOMY & MANAGEMENT PUBLISHING HOUSE

图书在版编目（CIP）数据

新时期中国商业银行 CSR 建设研究/朱文忠等著 . —北京：经济管理出版社，2016. 12
ISBN 978 - 7 - 5096 - 4841 - 4

Ⅰ.①新…　Ⅱ.①朱…　Ⅲ.①商业银行—企业责任—社会责任—研究—中国
Ⅳ.①F832. 33

中国版本图书馆 CIP 数据核字(2016)第 315174 号

组稿编辑：张　艳
责任编辑：张莉琼　高　娅
责任印制：黄章平
责任校对：超　凡

出版发行：经济管理出版社
　　　　　（北京市海淀区北蜂窝 8 号中雅大厦 A 座 11 层　100038）
网　　　址：www. E - mp. com. cn
电　　　话：(010) 51915602
印　　　刷：北京九州迅驰传媒文化有限公司
经　　　销：新华书店
开　　　本：720mm×1000mm/16
印　　　张：10. 5
字　　　数：181 千字
版　　　次：2016 年 12 月第 1 版　　2016 年 12 月第 1 次印刷
书　　　号：ISBN 978 - 7 - 5096 - 4841 - 4
定　　　价：39. 00 元

Abstract

Corporate Social Responsibility (CSR) refers to an enterprise's management philosophy that at the same time of creating profits to stakeholders it needs to assume responsibilities to its employees, customers, suppliers, community and society, including adhering to laws and regulations and business ethical principles, ensuring production safety and health, protecting labor benefits, protecting environments and natural resources, supporting philanthropy, and protecting disadvantaged groups, etc. CSR can be divided into four levels such as economic, legal, ethical and altruistic. Any business should be socially responsible, should not harm others and should create social benefits. In today's relationship era, an enterprise's actively taking social responsibilities to build a harmonious relationship with stakeholders like employees, customers, supplies and competitors, community and society is becoming a key factor for maintaining its long – term competitiveness and sustainability. In other words, an enterprise that creates benefits to society is actually creating benefits to itself. Otherwise, those firms that help others succeed will be more successful themselves. So it is necessary for modern businesses to integrate social responsibility targets into their ongoing business activities as a long – term strategy, which will ensure the long – term maximization of investors' benefits fundamentally.

Chinese commercial banks, especially the big four state – owned commercial banks, after their completion of shareholding reform, going public in both domestic and overseas markets and perfecting their corporate governance structures, tend to change their roles and business management goals from assuming the state's designed social responsibilities to maximizing their own profits or investors' benefits. In fact, there are really some problems appearing in their socially responsible behaviors such as unwillingness to make student loans, unfair charge of banking fees, supporting polluting enterprises with loans, or controlling real estate prices, etc. In this circumstance, it is of great importance for commercial banks to learn how to balance the interests of investors and those of other stakeholders in order to maintain their competitiveness. In addition, with the globalization of world economy and the internationalization of these banks, their stakeholders are becoming more and more diversified and enlarged. Therefore, it is of great value to rethink and reflect their CSR issue.

Research on the evaluation criteria and formation mechanism for Chinese commercial banks is of realistic significance. Firstly, the issue of CSR concerns about the sustainability of the banks. For instance, in the domestic market this issue may be an indicator for their increasing or declining reputation and image as well as sales performance while in overseas markets it may be a trade barrier for them to enter a new market. Secondly, commercial banks' CSR connotation and criteria differ from those of common enterprises, however, today there is not such a statement of connotation and criteria for the banks, so it deserves a specialized research on them. Thirdly, commercial banks' good performance in CSR is even more important in that they may drive or impact their borrowing customers to be socially responsible with their green lending policy, or they may directly impact the country's economic prosperity or social stability with their strong financing power.

Through the literature review and reflection of domestic and foreign CSR theories and practices, and the empirical study of commercial banks' current situation and problems in CSR management, and based on the conclusion of institutional pressure analysis and case studies that "institutional arrangement is more influencial than strategic benefits for an enterprise to drive a business to establish a good value of CSR", the paper puts forward a unique set of connotation and features for commercial banks' CSR, a unique set of criteria for evaluating their CSR performance, and a set of good mechanism for establishing their CSR cultural value. It is argued that due to the shortage of a complete internal and external corporate governance structure, in order to help Chinese commercial banks establish a sound CSR value, the legislative department is suggested to restrain commercial banks' business behaviors by perfecting the relevant laws and regulations, the government is suggested to direct them by designing and enforcing the related economic and social policies, the guild or NGO is suggested to regulate them by establishing an industrial standard, and the commercial bank itself is suggested to control themselves by establishing a diversified inner governance structure and to strengthen them by building a healthy environment of CSR corporate culture. It could be said that the perfection of Chinese commercial banks' internal and external corporate governance structures plays a key role for the formation of their good CSR value and performance.

Key Words: Chinese Commercial Banks; CSR Value; Connotation; Criteria; Mechanism

Contents

Chapter 1   Introduction

This chapter deals with relevant questions and the background, theoretical value, and realistic significance of the research and innovation points about CSR. And it will fully discuss the researching methods and ideas as well as the basic framework of the research.

1. 1   Research background and relevant questions

"Corporate Social Responsibility" (CSR) was first put forward by Oliver Sheldon of the UK in 1923. With the global human rights movement and environmental protection movement, CSR, influenced by the ideal of sustainable development, has enriched its substance and gained rising status. In recent years, the idea of "CSR" has drawn an increasing attention from the public. For example, *Fortune* and *Forbes* have both included CSR as one of their scoring criteria in the ranking of companies. In 2006, *People's Daily Online* and Chinese Culture Promotion Society organized the selection and awarding of those respected entrepreneurs and public trust brands with high social responsibility, and in 2012, China Central TV Financial Channel launched the top 50 index stocks with the consideration of five factors including social responsibility, which is a demonstration of the high value that China has placed on the CSR performance of Chinese companies.

Active fulfillment of CSR has become the shared strategic choice by more and more enterprises, because if a company couldn't deal with CSR properly from a strategic perspective, it is more likely to experience serious consequences, such as the bankrupcy of Sanlu Tainted Milk in China and the failure of Anron in the USA.

However, the theoretical study of CSR in China started later than that in the West, thus the specific study on relevant issues is not very perfect now. CSR echoes with cardinal virtues as "humanity, justice and harmony" in ancient Confucian culture and the doctrine of "Confucian businessman" in modern China. Those virtues are only the basis of ethical elements in social responsibility in modern Chinese corporations, while modern CSR reflects the attitude and is a practice of mature industrial democracy. In recent years, Being Globally Responsible Conference (BGRC) has launched in China and many CSR problems about Chinese enterprises were made public such as contractors dock workers' wages, land agents lift the housing price or the illegal labor employment of multinational companies. Therefore, Chinese academics started to pay much more attention to CSR and related researches. Some scholars thus have published relevant academic papers. For instance, Shi Yourong published a paper in *Wuhan University Journal* (*Social Sciences*) in 2002, and then Li Houhuan, Chai Gang, Chen Honghui, Zhu Wenzhong, and others all have published related research findings in the press or journal.

Although China has deeply studied CSR issue in some areas like coal, food and textile, researches on commercial banks' CSR are still in their infancy and have achieved little. People can find more academic papers on ordinary enterprises' CSR than on the CSR of the financial sector, especially that of commercial banks. In 2006, Zhang Youlong published a paper in *Studies of International Finance*, which is one of those rare. In addition, concrete results haven't reached in existing researches on the current situation, evaluation standards and mechanism construction of commercial banks' CSR. There are not such scholars who have made systemic and specific theoretical researches or empirical analysis on detailed issues on Chinese commercial banks including corporate values and performance, connotations and standards of CSR as well as how to promote their values.

However, it is of great significance to study on the CSR issue of commercial banks. The importance lies in that corporate values and performance of those banks not only involve their public image and sustainable development but influence the CSR performance of their clients and other social sectors and even the overall development of the whole national economy. Their CSR values have the "radiation" effect, which means it can produce effects on clients and other enterprises' CSR performance through "green credit" policy and investment philosophy (refusal to investment requirement from enterprises with high environmental pollution or those don't meet the CSR standard) . In the context of economic globalization and increasingly competitive market, CSR performance has been or is becoming a core competitive advantage for commercial banks in domestic and overseas markets. Hence, it is necessary to carry out a detailed research on commercial banks in this respect.

The core questions this research is expected to solve include:

Firstly, study and innovate the theoretical understanding of CSR. As we know, CSR is a self – regulatory mechanism under which shareholders benefit protection runs through all business activities. It is a process without ending point. Some misunderstandings need to be removed, such as, charitable contributions are equivalent to the firm's full implementation of all social responsibilities. And we can make some innovative research conclusions, such as, enterprises will fulfill more social responsibilities if being put more institutional pressure rather than strategic considerations.

Secondly, study and figure out the relationship between commercial banks' CSR and their sustainability. Some methods can help us verify their correlation and clarify the situation, problems and related causes of banks CSR. Those methods include questionnaire survey and qualitative analysis.

Thirdly, study and deal with specific connotations and evaluation criteria of commercial banks' CSR. How to define CSR connotations? What are detailed measures? What criteria are more suitable for banks's CSR evaluation? and so on.

Fourthly, study and address problems concerning the construction of values on CSR of commercial banks. Here is an example. A mechanism about commercial banks' CSR is needed to push forward the healthy and sustainable development of China's commercial banks and the overall financial sector so as to contribute to the building of a harmonious society, sound and rapid growth of national economy.

1. 2   Research significance

1. 2. 1   Theoretical significance

Taking a deep look at CSR theory is of great value. Since Oliver Sheldon's concept of "corporate social responsibility" was first put forward, relevant studies have been more and more profound particularly in recent China, but there are still some misinterpretations of CSR in the academic circle. Many just simply presume that "a company's economic strength is the premise", "to perform CSR is just money donation" or "the guarantee of CSR performance is SA8000 certification", and etc.. Actually, in its whole life cycle, a company needs to discharge its CSR at any time such as abiding by laws and regulations as well as moral norms. The only difference is that a company during its CSR performance can have different forms and emphasis. Besides, unlike in manufacturing, SA8000 standard couldn't apply to all financial service enterprises, and meanwhile, comprehensive studies are insufficient on the correlation between Confucian cultural values and modern CSR theory. So studies on theories about the CSR of contemporary commercial banks are. For these reasons, carrying out relevant theoretical researches is very significant.

1. 2. 2   Realistic significance

(1) The times and Chinese society call for deeper studies on CSR. As a heated topic, CSR issue in recent years has produced greater impact on companies' development, and social media have reported much more problems of CSR. Some problems are quite thought – provoking. For example, frequent coal – mine safety accidents have caused large casualties. Foreign fast – food brand like McDonald's and KFC's employ workers illegally or use overdue meat in fast – food production that infringes hourly workers rights and consumers' health. Factory inspections by foreign importers from time to time such as the so – called social audits affect exporters' competitiveness in the global market.

These phenomena indicate that many Chinese companies (including some famous multi-national companies) indeed neglect some problems which, if not handled properly, will directly influence not merely companies' sustainable development but also the social harmony and the development of social undertakings.

(2) Research on commercial banks' CSR is even more meaningful. Commercial banks, as special commercial enterprises, must shoulder more social responsibilities. On the one hand, commercial banks' CSR has different connotations and standards (they follow the "Equator Principles"), whose well CSR performance can protect social stability and national economic growth. Illegal behaviors of commercial banks could cause inflation and economic crisis (for instance, to issue loans without rational analysis will cause high multiplier effects and credit risks). On the other hand, commercial banks' values and performance on CSR have a sort of "radiation" effect on their clients and other enterprises. Commercial banks, through implementing green credit policy, can refuse to grant project loans to those companies that are substandard in pollution control. In this way, commercial banks can exert influence on the healthy development of all industries including manufacturing.

(3) There are indeed some CSR problems in modern commercial banks, which make a thorough research significant. There are some examples about commercial banks' CSR problems: arbitrary charges for services, plotting to bid up property prices with real state agencies, mandatory charges on loan collateral insurance with insurance companies and real state agencies. Many a problem reflects that we need to carry out research on and provide solutions to those problems in Chinese commercial banks.

1. 2. 3   Applications

After the review and reflection of CSR theories, this research, through field investigation and empirical analysis, will explore the status quo and problems of CSR in commercial banks both in China and abroad. The view that institutional rather than strategic considerations are preferred in setting up values on social responsibility in a company. The Stakeholder Theory has put forward a similar view. Based on this view, it is necessary to set up a set of unique CSR evaluation standards for commercial banks according to their features and introduce mechanisms that will lay the foundation of commercial banks' CSR. The standards and mechanisms to be properly used in the practice of CSR evaluation and ranking will play a positive role in the harmonious and sustainable development of commercial banks. They will also pose positive impact on building CSR values for other financial institutions.

1. 3 Research aim and methods

1. 3. 1 The aim of the research

Until now, Chinese commercial banks still don't have concrete evaluation standards or mechanisms in terms of CSR, even if some banks do have the standards, they are not arguable for wide availability. This research aims to innovate the theoretical knowledge by reviewing and rethinking CSR theories in China and other countries. Through questionnaire survey and case studies, we will also explore the status quo and problems of CSR in commercial banks both in China and abroad. According to The Stakeholder Theory and commercial banks' unique features, we will try to formulate a set of practical CSR standards and mechanisms that can help to establish their CSR values. In this way, commercial banks will contribute to the growth of the banking business and even the whole financial sector as well as the national economy.

1. 3. 2 The ideas of the research

China has carried out reform on property rights system including the stock system reform and stock listing of state – owned commercial banks. Some commercial banks as profit – seeking organizations, with governance structural flaws and economic performance dilemma, may neglect their social responsibilities due to the lack of government monitoring and the wrong value of profit maximization orientation in business operations. Therefore, those banks must learn the significance and the content of their CSR.

Here is an equation that shows how different commercial banks may take their CSR: CSR for the wholly state – funded banks = state and government instructions; CSR for joint – equity banks = own performance and management decisions. That means, after the property rights system reform, commercial banks themselves need to pay more attention to what their social responsibilities are. Besides, in "the era of relationship management", a company cannot achieve long – term success if it only depends on Scale Economy Effect, product and market – oriented strategies. It needs to take its social responsibilities, improve social benefits, adhere to business ethics and operate in accordance with laws. It can only maximize its long – term benefit and keep its core competitiveness if it contributes to all stakeholders and improves its relationship with all parties.

The basic thinking is here that: facilitated with relevant theories in management, economics and other subjects, this research will discuss issues such as business ethics and social responsibilities, laws, CSR, institutional motives and strategic motives in CSR. We will also put forward a set of standards and mechanisms unique for Chinese commercial banks based on an important conclusion that institutional elements play a key role in building corporate social responsibilities. The author thinks that during value concept construction, commercial banks require guidance from relatively sound law systems and government policies and collaboration with some industry associations and NGOs. It also needs to be controlled by multi – participated corporate governance structure and strengthened by a strong culture and moral environment. Our conclusion is that perfecting corporate governance structure will play a critical part in the establishment of commercial banks' CSR. Laws and regulations, government policies and NGOs in the industry are able to provide a sound environment for CSR establishment. In other words, they altogether set up legitimately an external corporate governance institution. Those banks' internal one will create an institutionalized running mechanism to incentive their sense of social responsibility.

1. 3. 3　Research methods

The research method is combing normative researches with empirical research. Methods like theoretical deduction, questionnaire survey and case study will be applied, data and materials are collected for quantitative and qualitative analysis. Thus we can make a profound analysis on issues related to commercial banks' CSR, standards and mechanisms in particular.

This research will carry out experimental studies. First, we will conduct questionnaire survey and analysis. In this case, we will distribute questionnaires to the staff of financial institutions and their clients in order to take a deep look at commercial banks' values, system arrangement and implementation on CSR. Second, we do case studies on several renowned commercial banks in developed countries with high CSR performance in order to sum up their practices and system arrangement. By means of studying on the influence of CSR performance in their sustainable development, we hope to acquire some enlightenment and lessons and verify the basic argument of this research.

1. 4　Research innovation

1. 4. 1　Theoretical innovation

This study raises that ancient Chinese Confucian culture has something to be learned for CSR values in contemporary enterprises. After review and reflection on foreign literature and theories on CSR, it also puts forward the basic ideas that "CSR will provide fundamental protection for the long – term benefits and sustainability of an organization" and "In building CSR values, institutional arrangement weighs more than strategic consideration". Put it simple, this research views that an organization's performance of CSR depends more on pressure from outside systems institutions (laws and regulations, policies and mechanisms and so on) than potential strategic benefits the organization will receive after social contributions. This view will guide the value – building for all corporations including commercial banks and provide theoretical basis for setting up a set of scientific CSR evaluation mechanisms for commercial banks.

1. 4. 2　Innovations in application

CSR benchmarks for commercial banks have been established according to practices by renowned western companies, policies and guidelines of the IFC and IM like the "Equator principles" by Zhang Changlong, and SA8000 set by the SAI as well as ISO26000 launched by ISO. Under such a context, this research formulates a concrete set of evaluation standards and a set of mechanisms for CSR value – building. Both those standards and mechanisms belong to the original achievements by this research, which are of great reference value for commercial banks and also other financial institutions in China.

1. 4. 3   Innovation in thinking

This research makes innovations in its research thinking: Due to some problems in governance structure of internal and external companies for Chinese commercial banks, legislature departments should gradually establish a set of law systems to monitor commercial banks' building of CSR values. Sound policies should be introduced, standards and management systems should be established by relevant industry associations and NGOs to guide and regulate as well. Commercial banks need sound corporate governance system and healthy corporate culture. In other words, the improvement of governance structure of internal and external companies will play a critical role in constructing CSR values.

1. 5   Research framework

The research will follow the following research framework as the general structure of logical thinking and the clear presentation of ideas as well as the clear arrangement of contents. Refer to Figure 1 – 1:

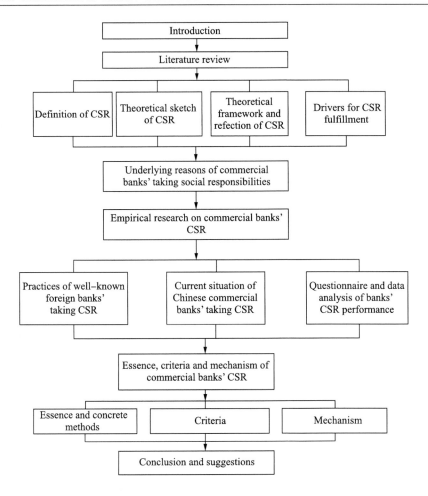

Figure 1 – 1   The logical analysis framework of the research

Chapter 2 Literature Review

In this chapter, we will make literature review on CSR definitions, theory skeleton and related studies in China and foreign corporations. Therefore, we can formulate theoretical frameworks and grounds for this research.

2. 1 Definition of CSR

Although there are expanding social responsibility movement around the world, richer connotation and more standards, there is no uniform international definition of it (Frankental, 2001). However, one thing is clear that basic elements of CSR should not only include shareholders, clients and staff benefits but also sustainable development, environmental protection and services for neighborhoods. On the other point of view, social responsibility is not just equivalent to setting up public image through donation or non – discrimination toward any group. Broadly speaking, it should keep harmonious ties between corporations and stakeholders, which means the companies need to encourage all stakeholders including clients to participate so as to meet people's demand and problems they encounter.

2. 1. 1 Definition of CSR by institutions

(1) Business for Social Responsibility defines CSR as "Operating a business in a manner that meets or exceeds the ethical, legal, commercial and public expectations that society has of business".

(2) The European Commission in 2001 defined it as "A concept whereby companies integrate social and environmental concerns in their business operations and in their

interaction with their stakeholders on a voluntary basis". There are two perspectives to define CSR: internal and external. Internal perspective means corporate performance on labor safety and health management, adaptability for changes, management on environmental protection and human resources (respect for diversity, employment discrimination, fair welfare treatment and training opportunities). External perspective indicates corporate concerns about investors, local community, business partners, suppliers as well as clients' benefits, human rights and global environment issue. Under the context of globalization, CSR tends to cover more areas like human rights. With the extensive global supply chain, Chinese companies' CSR will cover issues about human rights both domestically and abroad.

(3) The World Business Council for Sustainable Development (WBCSD) gives its definition: "Corporate Social Responsibility is the continuing commitment by business to behave ethically and contribute to economic development while improving the quality of life of the workforce and their families as well as of the local community and society at large. "

(4) The UNCTAD uses the definition that "CSR is an important element of our overall work programme, which seeks to bring together key stakeholders that can promote responsible international investment practices and contribute to sustainable development around the world".

(5) The USITC regards CSR as a company's promise to play its role in the society with responsible and sustainable approaches, the role including producer, employer, retailer, customer, citizen and etc.

(6) The World Bank provides a definition of business and the relationship between the key stakeholders, values, law – abiding and respect people, communities and the environment policies and practices relating to the collection. It is the company to improve the quality of life for stakeholders to contribute to sustainable development, a promise.

(7) An article by China Human Resources Management Research Institute points out that charity activities such as road and education donation as well as Hope Schools by corporations are not their main CSR. For companies, there are two main social responsibilities: one is the efficient use of social resources; the other is cultivating high – caliber personnel for our nation and society.

2. 1. 2   Definition of CSR by renowned companies and scholars

(1) Konosuke Matsushita, a world – famous entrepreneur thinks that a company's social responsibility includes three aspects: First, the company, on the basis of its own business, contributes to improving social life and happiness, which should be viewed as its fundamental mission. Second, the company should actively return its accumulated wealth to the society and the nation in all kinds of forms. Third, a company should reconcile all parties concerned and social problems including those caused by itself. All industries need to scrupulously abide by their duties and devote themselves to social progress (Li Haiming, 2003).

(2) Bloom and Gundlach believe that "The obligations of the firm to its stakeholders—people and groups who can affect or who are affected by corporate policies and practices. These obligations go beyond legal requirements and the company's duties to its shareholders. Fulfillment of these obligations is intended to minimize any harm and maximize the long – run beneficial impact of the firm on society" (Bloom and Gundlach, 2001).

(3) Rodriguez, Siegel, Hillman and Eden define CSR as instances where the company goes beyond compliance and engages in actions that appear to advance a social cause. Such actions might include adding social features or characteristics to products or modifying production processes to signify that the firm is seeking to advance a social objective (e. g. selling cosmetics with ingredients that are not tested on animals or adopting environmental – friendly technologies) or working closely with community organizations to ameliorate homelessness and indigence (e. g. the Society of St. Vincent De Paul). In an international context, CSR may also involve avoiding operations in countries that commit human rights violations (2006).

Chinese scholars also provide their definitions to CSR in various ways, for instance:

1) CSR, in addition to maximizing shareholders' profits, is the obligation to protect and promote public benefits (Liu Liping, 2006).

2) A company shows its responsibilities and obligations through institutions and conducts for relevant parties including employees, business partners, clients (consum-

er), community and even the country. That is CSR, which is the company's positive reaction to the market and party concerned and the comprehensive indicator of the company's performance (Yan Shengyong, 2006).

3) Corporate Social Responsibility refers to responsibilities to interested parties including stockholders (Zheng Mingcai, 2006).

4) When we talk about CSR, we mean that companies have the duty to extend their positive influence while limit negative influence to the society. CSR aims to maximize stockholders' profits, and maximize social benefits including those for workers, consumers, creditors, small and medium – sized companies competitors, the environment, disadvantaged social groups and the general public at the same time (Wang Dachao, 2005).

5) CSR, within the market economy system, means not only making profits for stockholders but also bringing other parties into consideration whose benefits affect and are affected by companies' behaviors (Luo Jianyan, 2006).

2. 1. 3   Tendency to consensus on CSR definition

According to opinions put forward by Wu Zhaoyun (2006) and the author, we have witnessed a tendency to consensus on CSR definition in the world in recent years. At present, there is a version that has been widely acknowledged: When making profits and shouldering responsibilities for stockholders, a company should also shoulder other responsibilities for its employees, consumers, suppliers, the community and the environment. Those responsibilities cover abidance by laws and regulations as well as business ethics, commitment to production security and occupational health and protection of workers' legitimate rights, environment and natural resources as well as support charity and disadvantaged social groups and so on.

According to the understanding and summarization of the author (2012), CSR can be defined as the following four types:

(1) As management philosophy, corporate social responsibility refers to the management philosophy that highlights both social benefits and economic interests in managerial decisions.

(2) As business practice, corporate social responsibility refers to the business prac-

tice to maximize profits and minimize negative impacts on the society at the same time.

(3) As evaluation system, corporate social responsibility is the evaluation system that considers profit – making, consumer satisfaction, and social wellbeing of the same value in assessing a firm's performance.

(4) As strategic goal, corporate social responsibility is the strategic goal of a firm that pursues the profit maximization through contributing to the society to enhance image and reputation in the long term.

2. 2   Theoretical skeleton of CSR

CSR originates from Europe and America in the 18th or 19th century. At that time, some companies took some ethic actions like equality, charity and better employment treatment, which were greatly influenced by religious ideas. In 1923, British Oliver Sheldon put forward the concept of "corporate social responsibility" formally. It has taken several decades for CSR basic framework from its building to a more mature, institutionalized and standardized one. In recent years, this idea has become increasing popular. For example, *Fortune* and *Forbes* have both included CSR as one of their scoring criteria in the ranking of companies. There is also the so – called "Confucian business-man" in modern China, but those ethic and moral factors of modern CSR are not norms. And companies are not conscious and willing to take their social responsibilities. Contemporary CSR ideas reflect the practice of mature industrial democracy (Lin Huasheng, 2005).

Contemporary CSR ideas only form and develop after the two world wars and escalating tensions of industrial and labor relations. Since the Second World War, labor union and other NGOs have emerged and mushroomed. Many standards and conventions have been adopted by the UN and other multilateral organizations focusing on human rights and environmental protection. Due to that, the concept of CSR can be spread and gradually become an internationally – acknowledge thought and an important element of international law system. The ideals about sustainable development pushed by global environmental protection movement also improve the spreading of CSR ideas.

In China, there are many thought – provoking issues about CSR. Some coalmine safety accidents impose threats on workers' lives. Some banks' declination to issue student loans bring unfavorable effects to poor students and our country's education. Some hospitals, disregard of professional morality, entrap patients. Construction companies' arrears of workers' salary harm workers' benefits. All those problems mirror the weakening CSR concept of our companies and such a tendency will affect the building of harmonious society in China. Since the convening of the BGRC in China in 2005, CSR has become the topic of people's discussions.

The theoretical skeleton and discussions concerning CSR can be generally summarized as the following.

2. 2. 1　Views from classical economics

The concept of CSR, if viewed from the perspective of economics, is an evolving concept, namely evolving from classical view or pure economic view to socioeconomic view. Milton Friedman (1973), representative of the classical view, he said in "The Social Responsibility of Business is to Increase its Profits" that: "There is one and only one social responsibility of business—to increase its profits. " In other words, Friedman believes that the only social responsibility for corporate executives is to maximize profits of owners or shareholders. However, what needs to be pointed out is that Friedman doesn't think companies should not take social responsibility, instead, he means that only the maximum of profits for shareholders is companies' social responsibility. He also mentioned that companies, in order to make profits, must produce those goods needed by the society in the most effective way on the premise of abidance with laws and moral norms. It will be beneficial for both companies and the society.

In fact, Friedman gets inspiration from ideas of "The Wealth of Nations" and "Invisible Hand" by Adam Smith. According to Adam Smith, driven by egoism, companies will pursue profits justifiably rather than create social benefits. In recent years, there are some classic economists that support CSR such as J. Henderson in 2007 and Albert Carr in his "Is Business Bluffing Ethical" in 1996.

2. 2. 2　Modern socioeconomic view

The socioeconomic view on CSR is that a company's executives should not only make profits but also protect and improve social welfare. In this aspect, a company, more than a financial institution, has responsibilities of contributing to its community and society as well as making profits. We can categorize scholars sharing this view into following:

(1) In 1930s, George Elton Mayo put forward three main values of businesses in *The Early Sociology of Management and Organizations* and *The Human Problems of an Industrial Revolution.*

(2) Ethical views on corporate operation: The so – called CSR indicates that companies, in addition to legal operation, should practice its ethical responsibilities that are equivalent to getting involved in profit – earning activities under the rule of laws. The general meaning of CSR covers statutory and ethical obligations (Li Zhenghua, 2005). A company should be regarded as an entity with ethical obligations, which is an inalienable part of its community. Benefits of the community and people should be taken into consideration (Hartman, 2001).

(3) Social network: Studies by socialists about "corporate social network production" reveal the law: Through expanding relevant networks, corporations can develop their corporate value chain. Corporations, by traditional charity activities based on altruism and commitments to traditional social responsibilities, will be able to incorporate potential stakeholders into the corporate social networks during their resource donations. Thanks to the above recognition, corporations will be devoted to charity and at the same time make themselves stronger in order to achieve the win – win goal. In other words, the aim of corporations' participation in charity is not only gaining their social influence and acknowledgment but promote their own competitiveness and sustainability.

(4) Corporate citizenship: It means that a company will combine its basic values with daily businesses practices, operation and policies. In this theory, companies, on the one hand, need to pay more attention to their own benefits; on the other hand, they should consider a fact that they belong to the society, that is "corporate citizens" and focus on long – term social benefits in order to be responsible for the whole society. It urges companies to deal with the relationship between corporate benefits and social ones appropriately, which will bring companies and the society into harmonious co – existence in effective ways.

All in all, although the above views are different in one way or another, they are common in one aspect that is purposes of business operation should not merely pursue e-conomic benefits but also the far – ranging social benefits. In this case, companies will be able to keep competitiveness in a long term and achieve sustainable and harmonious development.

2. 2. 3　Ancient confucian values

Core values of Confucianism reveal the quintessence of China's traditional culture with five thousand years of history, with benevolence, righteousness, faithfulness and others included. Those values can represent the values that sustain the balance of interests and harmonious development in the society. If we apply them into modern corporate management, they will help us build modern CSR values.

（1）Basic ideas of Confucianism. China boasts a civilization of 5000 years and Chinese people are deeply nurtured by Confucian culture. With the rapid development of Chinese economy, management circle has gained more interests in studying China's model of management and Chinese culture. Confucianism, evolving with the times, has exerted deep influence to corporate culture and ethics in China, not only in ancient times but also in modern eras. There are so – called Confucian businessmen in modern China whose business ethics and morals also affect China's business development and management philosophy. For example, having adopted ideas from Confucian culture, Haier advocates "The Interest Concept of Win – win Mode of Individual – Goal Combination". It also emphasizes harmony, self – discipline and group value, which help its success in markets both domestically and abroad. Some east and southeastern Asian countries also are nurtured by Confucianism, such as Japan, Singapore and the ROK. Confucian ideas on management based on family, kinship and collectivism influence the "loyalty" culture and management ideas featured by people – centered and comprehensive quality management in Japanese companies. Besides, such ideas also help the ROK publicize the contribution spirit that people should place the interests of the nation above their personal and group interests.

Generally speaking, Confucian culture, with Confucius, Mencius and Zengzi as its representative figures, is a traditional culture that focuses on humankind and harmonious interpersonal relationships. If we consider corporation management, we can bind those ideas like benevolence, righteousness and faithfulness with modern corporation management and operation so as to establish modern corporate management culture.

"Benevolence" is the so – called "kindheartedness" mentioned by Confucius in *Yan Yuan*. If we combine it with modern corporation management, it will help executives and managers adopt a kind of behaviors including treating workers well, bringing benefits for employers and doing charitable things for the public.

"Righteousness" refers to a quality for gentlemen to hold righteousness high in *Yang Huo*. It requires corporation managers to deal with appropriately the relationship between "righteousness" (social norms) and "interests" (material interests). Managers should let management ideas and practices meet moral requirements and interpret "interests" as "interests of all" rather than "interests of individuals". It requires corporations to put overall interests at their heart and pursue profits without harms to public interests.

"Harmony" directs at some philosophical ideas like "unity of nature and man" and "harmonious coexistence" in *Yi Jing* and the law of development that individuals, nations, societies and nature are interdependent and interactive. Companies should obtain some kind of equilibrium between self interests and social interests. If they blindly chase their own profits, such a profit will never be sustainable because of such a behavior violates harmonious co – existence. Therefore, in management process, leaders should make coordinated development between them and stakeholders such as employees and clients. During business process, they should also strive for win – win cooperation and achieve long – term development.

"Faithfulness" refers to moral codes: Loyalty, dedication to work and so on. Applying to modern enterprises, those codes mean sincerity among people, employees' dedication to work and employers' sincerity to clients and partners. Devotion to duty and honesty and trustworthiness are necessities for both individual growth and enterprises' development.

In addition, "manners and uprightness" upheld by Confucian culture also can be interpreted as principles in modern enterprises: "management of standardization" and "money – earning through honorable means".

(2) Possible links between Confucian culture and CSR values. The above discussions have indicated that there are close links between Confucian culture and modern CSR. Those links are as Table 2 – 1:

Table 2 – 1   The correlation between Confucian culture and modern CSR

Core values for traditional Confucian culture	Core values for modern CSR
"Benevolence" and "righteousness" mean bringing benefits for the society	CSR for the public: attention to charities to give back to the community and the society
"Benevolence" and "righteousness" mean care and protection for the subordinate	CSR for employees: attention to employees' health and security as well as social welfare
"Righteousness" and "honesty" mean making profits in a right way	CSR for clients: protection for consumers' legal rights and honest operation
"Harmony" means win – win cooperation	CSR for competitors: respect for competitors and partners, pursuit for win – win cooperation
"Manners" and "faithfulness" mean observance for rules and keeping promises	CSR for investors: abidance with laws and moral ethics in order to maximize investors' benefits

It is obvious to see the inner connection between the two. As a matter of fact, Confucian culture is the resource of early ethic factors and thinking of modern CSR.

Firstly, "benevolence" and "righteousness" advocated by traditional Confucian culture including moral habits such as the whole benefit exceeds the individual one. Such habits echo the content of "corporate social responsibility for the public", which always manifests as: companies should care about public health and care, support charity, conserve natural environment and create more jobs as well as reward their communities.

Secondly, "benevolence" and "righteousness" also contain moral behaviors to the subordinate, which is in accordance with "corporate social responsibility for employees". The practices are focusing on workers' security, health, life quality, working environment and reasonable pay as well as care for workers in difficulties and providing insurance to them covering medical care, accident insurance and retirement pension.

Thirdly, "righteousness" and "uprightness" reflect the operation rule of making money through honorable means. Confucianism lays much more importance on uprightness than on interests, and it has an ideal of equal society. So does "corporate social responsibility for clients". According to this idea, modern companies need to hold accountable for their clients and take honorable means to make profits in case of cheating on clients. Consumers' rights to be informed and to be heard should be protected by companies.

Fourthly, "harmony" can indicate the harmonious relationship of companies with their partners and competitors and within their workers. This view is closely linked with "corporate social responsibility for competitors and partners". When in competition, companies should hold the view of "harmonious co – existence" in order to achieve the win – win situation through fair play and cooperation.

Fifthly, "manners" and "loyalty" indicate the operation thinking of "abidance with regulations and laws" and the code of "honesty and sincerity". This matches to corporate social responsibility for investors. Companies can create profits for their investors by doing business, but they should not be engaged in illegal operation, and destroying social morals. It is their duty to operate according to laws and regulations while at the same time, comply with social morality and pursue for sincerity. It will fundamentally protect investment interests for their investors and guarantee their own competitiveness in the long – term.

(3) Reference and enlightenment. Through the above discussion, we have noted that there are connections between traditional Confucian culture and modern CSR.

Firstly, Confucian culture supports the development of values of CSR that is based on, so to speak, preeminent western and oriental management thinking integrated with Chinese Confucian culture and Japanese corporate culture. Theory Z put forward by William Ouchi in the 1980s, is a typical example of the eastern culture. In other words, Confucian culture promotes the form of modern CSR, which can be revealed from the economic practice of Japan and "Asia's Four Little Dragons" in modern times. We can take a closer look at such an influence. The idea of "honesty and integrity" of Confucian culture is similar to that in modern CSR values. The Confucian idea of "harmonious co – existence between nature and humankind" is more appropriate than "egoism and fierce competition" for modern corporations. The idea held by Confucian culture that collective benefits far weigh than individual benefits is supplementary to western individualism. Institutionalized management thoughts can be improved by Confucian moral ideas and spiritual fruits. Confucian culture focuses on moral responsibilities for the society, which are more demanding than economic and legal social corporations. The law of business is morality. Humanitarian management model will mobilize employees more effectively than institutional control. Some western companies generally speak a lot about institutional management and control, that is legalism. This practice, however, is not always appropriate especially in oriental countries like China that advocates "the rule of man". Therefore, combining values of Confucian culture with western corporate values will create better modern CSR values with wider range of applicability.

Secondly, Confucian values exert a long – term influence on every aspect of modern CSR values. For instance, in terms of corporate management, Confucian culture is centered on humankind as well as collective strength. It can be applied to help modern companies foster the concept of "humanitarian management". On the one hand, the concept can make companies focus on customers, workers and shareholders. On the other hand, it can encourage collective wisdom in order to give workers' initiative full play, meet customers' demands and finally maintain sound development of companies. In terms of corporate values, the idea of "keeping balance between uprightness and interests" can enlighten companies to efficiently link profits – earning with social effects. A company should try its best to serve and reward its communities and the general public so as to promote its public image and make external environment favorable for development. As far as competition ideas are concerned, harmony should be cherished, so companies should stick to the principle of win – win cooperation in competition. As to the code of conduct, the principle of "honesty and integrity" has asked companies to treat clients with sincerity and meet word with deeds. Malfeasance like providing fake and poor quality commodities should be banned. To sum up, Confucian values are similar to modern CSR values in each aspect. The former is the core and resource of the moral part of the latter.

Thirdly, it is significant to inherit and view Confucian values in a critical and dialectical way. Although Confucian values make up the "management of Chinese style" and lay cultural foundation for east Asian economic miracles, we must notice that every coin has two sides, so Confucian values in some degree are conservative and passive. Its spirit – oriented values contradict with materialism in the West. Westerners believe material benefits are necessary for social progress and personal values. Opinions such as "contentment is happiness" and "Anatman" will adversely affect entrepreneurship and pursuit of excellence for modern businessmen. "The rule of man" advocated by Confucianism may be in conflict with "the rule of law". Western culture pinpoints the rule of law and its forces on people's conducts, while Confucianism stresses on harmonious relationship and the function of moral persuasion. The concept of "the rule of man" will do no benefits for the market economy which requires fair competition and operations according to laws.

2.3　The theoretical framework and reflection of CSR

After discussing the basic concept, definition and literature review of CSR theory, we can conclude that a responsible company should maximize its positive effects meanwhile minimize its adverse effects on the society. We believe the following recognition and reflection really matters.

2.3.1　CSR means high attention to the profit of stakeholders

Friedman said that the primary stakeholder of concern in business decision making is the stockholders/owners, subscribers to the idea of a corporate social contract also take the short – term and long – term interests of other parties into account. Social contract theorists observe that business decisions often impact large numbers of individuals, groups or institutions. Stakeholders include any individuals or groups affected by the organization's actions, policies and decisions (they have a stake in the outcome of the company's decisions), as well as any individual or group who is vital to the survival and success of the enterprise (Freeman, 2001). But it neglects those of other stakeholders. Actually, the concept of stakeholders covers a wide range of parties including those influenced by a company's activities and policies and those important for a company's survival and development such as owners, workers, local community and the general public.

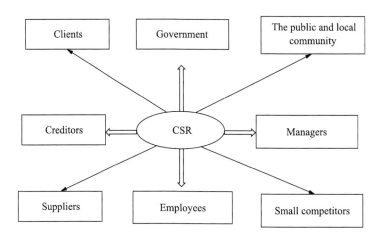

Figure 2 – 1   Stakeholders of CSR

Among related parties, owners, creditors, managers and workers can be called as internal stakeholders, clients, the general public and local community as well as suppliers and small competitors external stakeholders (see Figure 2 – 1). We must note that there may be some overlapping in the so – called internal and external stakeholders. For example, managers and workers may hold their company's stocks together so that they are also owners or shareholder; clients may belong to the local community. Besides, there is a clarification of some stakeholders: managers and workers can be called as employees while owners and creditors investors.

Recently, some Chinese scholars have done similar researches on stakeholder classification. Chen Xun (2005) and Jiang Ruochen (2006) have respectively made hierarchical and category – based models. Based on their researches, the author believes we can classify stakeholders into Table 2 – 2 according to definition, duty degree, contractual relationship, ownership and inside or outside the institution.

Table 2 – 2   Shareholders of CSR

Number	Basis of classification	Classification	Notes
1	Definition range	General definition	Anyone or group that can affect companies operation such as stockholders, suppliers, employees and related organizations and etc.
		Specific definition	Anybody or group that has direct relations with companies such as managers, clients and competitors
2	Responsibility level	Primary level	Stockholders, creditors, managers and employees
		Middle level	Clients, suppliers and government departments
		Senior level	Social organizations and groups and competitors
3	Contractual relationship	Complete	Stockholders and managers
		Incomplete	Employees, creditors, clients and government departments
		None	Social organizations and competitors
4	Within and outside organization	Within	Managers and employees
		Outside	Stockholders, creditors, clients, suppliers and competitors
5	Property relations	Main bodies	Stockholders, creditors, managers and employees
		Non – main bodies	Clients, suppliers, government departments and competitors

The above chart indicates that the definition of CSR should be comprehensive and hierarchical. Companies' responsibility should be determined in line with their condition and relationship with stakeholders. Companies needn't take all responsibilities in the same way. However, as we know, stakeholders' conducts in a company will affect the fulfillment of its goals in this or that way. And some of them like workers and clients are critical for a company's success. It is not hard to imagine results if a company doesn't care about those stakeholders' interests. And the best solution to this issue is that companies need to balance interests of all parties concerned instead of owners.

Moreover, Lantos (2001) believes that "stakeholders can be envisioned as existing at four levels. First level is the systemic, macro – environmental, general environment level – larger societal factors, including the entire business system, the social system, plus society at large, which consists of institutions and forces, such as economic, legal, political, technological, natural, media and socio – cultural forces. The second level of stakeholders is the corporation's micro – environment/operating/task environment—its immediate environment, consisting of exchange relationship partners (such as suppliers and distributors), plus competitors, customers, the local community and the financial community (stockholders, bondholders, and creditors). A third level of stakeholders is found within the business organization, notably superiors, subordinates and other employees and labor unions. The final level of stakeholder is significant for others of business decision makers, such as peers, family, friends, etc." (Lantos, 2001).

As early as in 1984, R. Edward Freeman made discussions on this aspect. In the book of *Strategic Management: A Stakeholder Approach*, Friedman firstly introduced the analysis of stakeholders into management and defined stakeholders as individuals and organizations influence or are influenced by corporate operation and activities. In the author's view, such an innovative theory injects a new way of thinking for corporate managers, which identifies and models the groups which are stakeholders of a corporation, and both describes and recommends methods by which management can give due regard to the interests of those groups. In short, it attempts play to address the "Principle of Who or What Really Counts." Companies can pay attention to environmental protection and charity to protect the public's benefits and provide products with high quality and security level to protect interest of clients. Other measures like fair welfare and safe working environment as well as strategic partnership can also create benefits for employees and suppliers etc. Companies build sound relationship with other parties and promote social image, which will create win – win result and reach long – term growth.

2.3.2 CSR is a strategic goal for corporate long – term development

(1) Social responsibility is the cornerstone of companies' long – term development. Simply, profit – maximizing should not be the only target of a company. Its targets should at least cover five areas including CSR as an important strategic target (see Figure 2 –2).

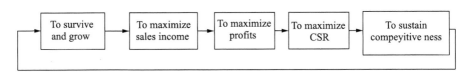

Figure 2 – 2   Types and correlations of companies' operation goals

Good corporate conducts will be good to companies and the whole society. Strategic philanthropy is rooted in profit motive (Quester and Thompson, 2001). Many people think strategic CSR will increase companies' burden and costs and reduce efficiency. It is true in the short term. However, in the long run, with strengthened social responsibility, companies can improve public image and in turn create a more favorable environment and more profitable market so that their profits will increase and lay a solid foundation for its profit – maximizing effort and competitiveness. The core reason for companies to shoulder social responsibility is that it comes hand in hand with companies' growth and sustainability.

According to corporate life cycle, a company should adjust timely their key social responsibility along with its own development. In its early stage, survival is its priority. And when it is in mature stage with increasing relative benefits and gaining more strength, it should focus on performing its social responsibility voluntarily. While it is in a declining phase, it should control adverse effects caused by switching to other production areas and bankruptcy, which is relatively relaxed social responsibility.

(2) The correlation between CSR and corporate sustainable development. Generally speaking, social responsibility will inevitably increase a company's costs, which is in conflict with its profit – maximizing goal. However, many studies have shown that there is a positive correlation between CSR and corporate economic results.

1) Many scholars have raised their analysis for reasons behind such a positive correlation. According to Wang Dachao in 2005 and Zhu Wenzhong (2012, 2015), taking responsibility will improve economic benefits for companies. First, the performance of responsibilities for employees will motivate employees and increase their senses of belonging and loyalty in order to gain higher efficiency. Second, the fulfillment of responsibilities for clients and suppliers will win favorable impression and trust for companies. Third, responsibilities for the general public will enhance reputation and brand awareness. Finally, it is more likely to create win – win cooperation and reduce competition risks and costs if companies could take responsibilities for companies' competitors. All these factors will have a direct effect on companies' performance.

Shi Jinping and Wang Shuang in 2006 said that costs will be reduced if companies could take their social responsibilities. First, it would avoid having conflicts with stakeholders. Second, it will help set up public image and win customers support and trust. Third, it will gain popularity among workers and incentivize them. Forth, it will promote companies' ties with suppliers and gain preferential terms of delivery. Fifth, the relationship with government will get better so that companies will be able to win more supports and fewer barriers from government.

2) Based on conclusions of model analysis, there indeed is a positive correlation between CSR and sustainable development. Wang Jingjing and Zhang Fei in 2003 expressed that from the perspective of Game Theory, we can consider long – term cooperation between companies and stakeholders and how such cooperation will affect companies' development. Provided that both a company and its stakeholders are rational, the best option for every party depends on others' strategic choice. If the market exchange just happens once, a company will never consider actively shouldering social responsibility or establishing positive partnership. Coase theorem affirms that where there are complete competitive markets with no transactions costs, an efficient set of inputs and outputs and production – optimal distribution will be selected, regardless of how property rights are divided. It believes that when property rights are involved, parties naturally gravitate toward the most efficient and mutually beneficial outcome.

According to model analysis, let us suppose there are two periods and two participants (company manager and a stakeholder) in a company. We set π as the profit for the second period that is evenly distributed in the interval $[0, \theta]$. The manager knows θ while the stakeholder only knows the probability distribution of θ as $\mu(\theta)$. In Period 1, managers choose certain social activities as A. Due to insufficient information, the stakeholder can only decide the market value as V_0 by predicting A. In Period 2, the company realizes its profit goal that here we set as the weighted average of the market value in Period 1 and the expectation value in Period 2 (except social participation costs):

$$\mu(A, V_0(A), \theta) = (1 - r) V_0(A) + r[\theta/2 - C \times A/2]$$

$V_0(A)$ is the market value of the company in Period 1 with social participation of A. $\theta/2$ is the expectation value in Period 2. $C * A/2$ represents the social cost of the company when participating in social activities with r as the weight. The objective function reflects a supposition that the welfare of a company's manager increases with increasing company market values and decreases with the increasing of social costs.

　　When the manager chooses social participation level as A, he predicts that the stakeholder will choose V_0 (θ) . If the manager chooses A while the stakeholder believes the expectation of Q – type is $\overline{Q}(A)$, the company's market value will be :

　　$V_0(A) = \overline{Q}(A)/2$

　　There is a formula as: $\alpha^2(A, V_0(A), \theta)/ \alpha A \; \alpha\theta = r*c/ \theta^2 > 0$. In this formula, we can see that if the company has a better quality (θ), it will be more likely to take part in social activities. It echoes with the Spence – Mirrlees separating equilibrium. If we substitute V_0 (A) in Effectiveness Function and take a derivative of A, we can deduce the first order condition as:

　　$\alpha u/ \; \alpha A = [1/2 \, (1-r)] \; * \; [2\alpha(A)]/2A - r*c*(1/\theta) = 0$

　　In equilibrium case, investors can deduce from A directly to θ. In other words, if $A(\theta)$ is the best option for the manger of θ – type company, then $\tilde{\theta}[\; A(\theta) \;] = \theta$. Hence, $(\alpha \, \tilde{\theta}/\alpha A) = (\alpha A/ \; \alpha\theta)^{-1}$. If we substitute this equator in the first order function, we will get a differential equation:

　　$2r*c* \; (\alpha A/ \; \alpha\theta) - (1-r) = 0$

　　Solve it and will get $A(\theta) = [\;(1-r)/ 4rc] \; * \; \theta^2 + C_1$

　　The above equation is the equilibrium strategy for manager. If we reverse the formula and substitute θ in $V_0 = (\theta/2)$, we will get the company's market value as:

　　$V_0(A) = \{ \; (A - C_1) \; * \; [\;(r*c)\;] \; \}^{1/2}$

　　In this game, due to successively distributed type θ without non – equilibrium case, there will be a posteriori probability for every A by Bayes Law as $\tilde{\mu}(\theta^{-1}) \; (A)/ A = 1$ and $\tilde{\mu}(\tilde{\theta} \neq \theta^{-1})(A)/A = 0$. $(\theta^{-1}) \; (A)$ represents the inverse function of manager equilibrium strategy as $A(\theta)$.

　　The aforesaid Bayes equilibrium indicates the higher quality a company is, the more willing to participate in social activities. Even the stakeholder can't observe a company's quality but can observe whether it takes part in social activities in the long run. The stakeholder will decide whether to form long – term partnership with the company. Through taking on social responsibility, a company can win the stakeholder's good sense, driving for its long – term benefits and sustainable development.

　　Studies both in China and abroad have shown that CSR keeps a positive correlation with companies financial performance, which means that in most cases, CSR could promote financial performance and then creates a better environment for sustainable development. For example, Guo Hongling (2006) concluded research results of 11 papers since 1997 and discovered that 7 of 11 showed CSR has positive influence on companies' financial performance. As a result of the author's recent collection of related researches, in the total of 83 papers under research, 62% of those believe the relationship is positive (see Table 2 − 3). Based on the analysis, it is easy for us to see that active performance in social responsibility will be conducive to companies' real economic results and further their capacity for sustainable development.

Table 2 − 3   The correlation between CSR performance and financial performance

Group studied	The number of articles	The number of positive effects	The number of no effects	The number of negative effects
1	21	12	8	1
2	51	33	9	9
3	11	7	2	2
Total/Proportion(%)	83	62	22	14

3) More importantly, in terms of commercial banks, Simpson and others carried out research about the relationship between CSR performance and financial performance in 1993 − 1994 for all commercial banks in the United States. They evaluated those banks by the ranking of Community Reinvestment Act and financial performance with return on total assets and credit loss rate. They found there is a positive correlation in the area of commercial banks. Therefore, the way of better financial performance through active CSR is also applied to commercial banks.

In conclusion, companies, with active role in social responsibility, can improve their public image and economic results so as to promote their competitiveness and their boost sustainable development.

2. 3. 3   CSR emphasizes ethical responsibility

Ethical social responsibility has different definitions in many countries and companies. The widespread acceptable principles for commercial ethics are avoiding harm to others, showing respects for others' rights and fulfilling contractual obligations, etc.

In the US, ethical CSR has many development stages, each with different focuses. Its development is progressive. According to Table 2 – 4, it shows that CSR has different focuses in the past 100 years in the US. In the early stage of 20th century, religious values were laid great importance due to their guidance on protection of profits for clients, competitors and workers. In the late 20th century, CSR focused on abidance with government laws and regulations. In the 21st century, CSR focused on how international law and moral norms could protect benefits for a wider range of stakeholders in the global market.

Table 2 – 4　The social development of the United States and changes in CSR moral focuses

Time	Historical event	Social responsibility stage	Moral focus
Before 1900	Industrial mass production	Not yet formed	Traditional thinking and patriarchy governance mode
1910s	Ford sociology	The first stage	Ford religious values
1930s	The Great Depression	The first stage	Individualistic heroism and obedience to supervision
1940s	The Second World War	The first stage	Support for wars
1950s	Recovery to normal development	The first stage	Profits – earning
1960s	The big society	The second stage	Predominance of federal government
1970s	Construction of social law systems	The second stage	Transformation and obedience to laws
1980s	Corporate moral loss	The third stage	Corporate social contribution
1990s	Test of moral ethics	The third stage	Obedience to regulations and protection of public images
2000s	Globalization	The fourth stage	Observance with local laws and environmental protection

Note: The chart is based on the articles published by Knouse and others.

There are three influential management researchers in the US history: Frederick Winslow Taylorh, Chester Barnard and Peter F. Drucker. We should note that they all made explanation or interpretation on commercial ethics and moral norms in corporate management. Frederick Taylor was one of the intellectual leaders of the Efficiency Movement and the ideas he put forward were highly influential in the Progressive Era. In *The Principle of Scientific Management in* 1911, Taylor, often called as "The Father of Scientific Management", discussed many commercial ethics in details like employee satisfaction, social benefits and others related to workers' interests. Chester Barnard, in *The Function of the Executive*, told cooperation mechanism for formal corporate institutions. In which, he mentioned time and again commercial ethics in CSR such as one of the most important functions for managers are coordinate workers' wishes with companies' goals. Besides, leadership in a company needs to establish sound ethics and play a leading role. Peter Drucker (1980), "the founder of modern management", puts forward many commercial ethical questions in works like *Concept of the Corporation*. He supports power delegation and focuses on the ethical judgment of delegated managers. He puts forward MBO (management by objective) and the issue of achieving the purpose of using unscrupulous divisive tactics. In Drucker' views, there are three ethical social responsibilities: the pursuit of profits should not be the only operation goal; companies, as social institutions, have social responsibility; companies have special social responsibility for their employees.

In China, many businessmen regard CSR as ethical responsibility beyond legal obligations. The CEO of Dupont China Holding Co. , Ltd. , John Brown, when was asked about which matters more – performance or ethics, said on the one hand his company believes, performance matters, but on the other hand, if a company wants to achieve long – term development, it should own core values and be ethical.

Legal obligations are the social responsibilities stipulated by laws and administrative laws for companies. Laws stipulate companies must protect their customers, environmental protection and employees' benefits such as *Law of the People's Republic of China on Product Quality* and *Law of the People's Republic of China on Environmental Protection*, etc. But laws can't cover all details and couldn't be applied to all circumstances. Laws stipulate what people must and can't do something but lack willingness. They are mandatory rather than voluntary.

In the contrast, ethical social responsibility refers to what are required to be conducted for companies in ethical and moral norms, with honest operation, fair workers' salaries and attention to the public health included. It is notably that ethical social responsibility is not mandatory and the fulfillment relies on companies' initiatives and capability. Therefore, the main work to promote CSR should be in the area of ethical social responsibility that is also the focus of CSR.

2.3.4　The fulfillment of CSR is the process management with open ending

The fulfillment of CSR is not a temporary social contribution activity but a process management without ending, which means it should go through the whole operation process of companies. Companies can't wait and perform responsibility until they have attained enough profits. As a matter of fact, this research believes that CSR should be in every stage of companies' performance and operation. For instance, at its very start, a company will show whether it fulfills its social responsibility like offering real information and avoid misleading authorities. And then its production activities will also reveal its responsibility such as environmental protection and ecological balance. Its commercial exchanges will show whether it protect customers' legitimate rights. When the company gets richer, it should also fund charity and the disadvantaged group. Meanwhile, a company needs to care its responsibility for employees including employment discrimination and fair and reasonable welfare treatment.

2.3.5　Four levels and four stages of CSR

There are 4 levels and 4 stages concerning CSR and each step forward symbolizes a leap for CSR. Concrete and obvious order exists in CSR that always goes through all companies' operation. According to the degree of mandate, CSR can be divided into four levels and stages (see Figure 2 – 3).

Figure 2 – 3   Four levels of CSR based on Lantos (2001)

(1) Economic responsibility: According to the table, economic and social responsibility lie in the bottom. The position suggests that the first responsibility for companies is to make profits for stakeholders and investors, forming the foundation for other social responsibility. In the previous years, Novak (1996) had more fully delineated a set of seven economic responsibilities: ① Satisfy customers with goods and services of real value; ② Earn a fair return on the funds entrusted to the corporation by its investors; ③ Create new wealth, which can accrue to non – profit institutions which own shares of publicly – held companies and help lift the poor out of poverty as their wages rise; ④ Create new jobs; ⑤ Defeat envy though generating upward mobility and giving people the sense that their economic conditions can improve; ⑥ Promote innovation; ⑦ Diversify the economic interests of citizens so as to prevent the tyranny of the majority.

(2) Legal responsibility: Means companies should comply with laws, undertake legal obligations and do business based on market rules. The introduction of laws and regulations to regulate companies' operation attributes to the society can't ensure companies to operate at good will at all time. In fact, phenomena such as the violation of laws and unscrupulous business activities occur frequently in the market.

(3) Ethical responsibility: Indicates that companies should follow commercial ethics and the principle of sincerity. Ethical social responsibility, although not written into law, could be not only encouraging policies and practices but policies that will ban and prevent people from being involved in. This responsibility originates from religious be-

liefs, ethical norms, humanitarian codes and human rights (Novak, 1996). It is wide-ly acknowledged that ethical responsibility should be in the third position. However, not all companies practice it in business.

(4) Voluntary responsibility: Lies in the top of this hierarchy. Under that, compa-nies want to behave as a good participant of the society and will support charity and com-munity programs through donation. Charitable actions and donations are always inter-twined with public relations activities. As part of Strategic CSR, charitable responsibility is often regarded as a marketing tool to improve companies' public image and better ful-fill economic responsibility.

Among the above four kinds of CSR, economic and legal responsibilities are re-quired by the society. Ethical responsibility is expected, and voluntary one is hoped by the society. In this hierarchy, the higher a company reaches, the higher of its sense of social responsibility is.

Besides, CSR can be divided into four stages according to the knowledge of compa-nies' managers. The stage of attention: to ownership and managers; to workers; to spe-cific environmental members and constituents; to wider society (see Figure 2 –4).

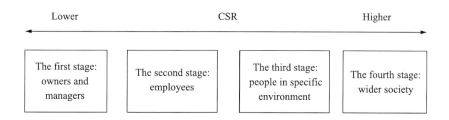

Figure 2 –4   Four stages of CSR

Note: This framework is adapted based on ideas of Robbins and Coutler (2002).

This model reveals how managers progressively know more about social responsibili-ties and the level of social responsibilities. Put it in simple words, managers' recogni-tion of CSR values depends on whom they think should be the target for their responsibili-ties.

In the first stage, the only aim for managers is maximizing profits for owners and themselves without considering to meet others' demands. It is the classical CSR value advocated by Friedman (1973). In the second stage, managers are committed to focusing on human resources in order to encourage good workers. Hence, managers will make great efforts to improve workers' working conditions, participation and sense of security. In the third stage, the target will be expanded to stakeholders in certain environments such as clients and suppliers. Managers are eager to achieve fair prices, high – quality, secure products and services, good relationship with suppliers, etc. The last stage is also the highest where managers recognize the necessity to expand social responsibility. Companies will be viewed as Public Entity and Corporate Citizenship who must promote social benefits for all. Under this circumstance, managers will improve social justice, protect environment and support social and cultural activities. They will stick to it even costs will increase and profits will decrease.

Similarly, according to Figure 2 – 4, from the left to the right, every stage ahead indicates a leap in managers' CSR values. We must admit that the fundamental social responsibility for managers is complying with laws, regulations and profit – earning. Ignoring either of them will impose threats on corporate survival. But there are other stakeholders and they will help managers focus on key issues and make better decisions.

2.3.6　Confucian culture in building modern CSR values

As mentioned above, Confucian culture supports the development of exert long – term influence on every aspect of modern CSR values. Confucian values are the core resource of the moral part of the latter. It is significant to inherit and view Confucian values in a critical and dialectical way.

2.3.7　Misunderstandings should be cleared up in forming CSR values

(1) Misunderstanding 1: CSR is the same as charitable donations. Companies will perform their social responsibilities in the way of charitable donations, but they are far beyond that. We can know the connotation of CSR from following aspects. First, from the aspect of CSR level, charitable activities are only the highest level of CSR as voluntary responsibility. What makes voluntary responsibility so special is that with stronger economic power, companies can make more contributions. Second, in terms of benefici-

aries of CSR, charitable actions bring benefits for the public, but CSR has more stakeholders like clients, investors and workers. Furthermore, charitable actions are just one way so companies need to take actions in other areas such as social security, health, environment and education and so on. And finally, if we look at the recognition stage of companies, charitable actions only indicate that companies are in the fourth stage. The first stage is that the only goal of companies is to maximize profits for their ownership and themselves rather than meet demands for others. The second stage is that managers are committed to being responsible for their employees. Those responsibilities cover many areas such as expanding employees' welfare and participation as well as increasing job security. The third stage is that corporate social responsibilities cover more stakeholders like clients, suppliers and competitors in the market. The fourth stage is the highest form of CSR in socioeconomics. Overall speaking, it is not appropriate to equate CSR with charitable donation.

The potential risk of such a misunderstanding or wrong conception is that for companies managers, they may think that companies which have done enough charitable or philanthropical responsibilities have already fulfilled their social responsibilities. It is likely that those managers could ignore more social responsibilities, which can adversely affect formulating positive CSR values.

(2) Misunderstanding 2: The premise of fulfilling social responsibilities is that a firm itself is wealthy. We must admit that a company's economic strength will decide, to some degree, whether it can take its social responsibility or not. If a company with great debt and loss, it will be unrealistic to require a company to shoulder social responsibilities related to money such as helping community orphans, paying high salaries and welfare for workers. But just as we have discussed before, CSR has different levels and stages. In the different stage of life cycle, a company must fulfill its social responsibilities, only with various focuses and differences. As a matter of fact, since a company registers, it has social responsibilities because at that time, the application report must be to the truth, which is a moral responsibility for the company. It also needs to shoulder legal responsibilities during its ongoing operation, such as operation in accordance with the law and no customer fraud. There are other social responsibilities in a company's life cycle which include fair employment, protecting environment and implementing statutory

minimum wage. Another kind of basic social responsibilities is economic responsibilities, that is, a company must create benefits for its stockholders and investors in the market economy. But at the same time, it should take social responsibilities of moral and legal types in order to make sure the security and maximum of stockholders' investment. All in all, if we say that only when companies have strong economic power can they fulfill social responsibilities, it is unreasonable and misinterpreted in some way.

Similarly, this misunderstanding will potentially provide an excuse of limited economic power for managers to give a cold shoulder to other social responsibilities. Such a neglection will lose the cornerstone of sustainable development. They will fail in achieving everlasting success and famous admirable brands.

(3) Misunderstanding 3: The guarantee for CSR fulfillment is to be certified with SA8000. SA8000 surely is a globally recognized standard for CSR. Most of exporters need to get this certification to make sure their export business. It is an auditable certification standard, developed in 1997 by Social Accountability International (SAI), that encourages organizations to develop, maintain, and apply socially acceptable practices in the workplace. But it is not the only standard for CSR. First, SA8000 is an international certification system, which aims to protect labor forces such as how to guarantee working environment and condition for workers. It measures the performance of companies in eight areas important to social accountability in the workplace: child labor, forced labor, health and safety, free association and collective bargaining, discrimination, disciplinary practices, working hours and compensation. This system doesn't cover corporate social responsibilities for investors, clients and communities. Second, it only applies to manufacturing – type enterprises rather than to all enterprises. Few service – oriented enterprises like banks, insurance, securities and consulting attain this certification. From the above, we can see that SA8000 is not a CSR standard adopted by all companies.

There are international certification systems for social responsibility standards like ISO9000 and ISO14000 as well as ISO26000 related to clients and the public rights. Financial sector has its own CSR standard like the Equator Principles. The Equator Principles is a risk management framework, adopted by financial institutions, for determining, assessing and managing environmental and social risk in project finance. Until now, more than 100 major banks in the world such as HSBC, Citigroup and ABN have adopted this system and deliver debts to only those companies up to social standards and standards on environmental protection. Even if a company is certificated with SA8000 and then operates according to this standard, we can't say and confirm it has fulfilled its social responsibilities. In other words, there is a misunderstanding if regarding SA8000 as the guarantee for CSR fulfillment.

If managers have such a misunderstanding, they are more likely to think their companies have taken and fulfilled all the social responsibilities, and they needn't consider other responsibilities.

(4) Misunderstanding 4: CSR will only increase costs. If a company performs its social responsibilities, those projects like improving worker welfare and investing in community service and environmental protection, all will increase the company's costs. And a company usually can't see what direct marginal benefits can be brought by the costs in the short term. There is a time – lag effect in the influence of CSR on economic performance within a company. Researches in China and beyond have shown that in the long term, there is a positive correlation between positive performance of CSR and financial results. *The Corporate Social – Financial Performance Relationship: A Typology and Analysis* by Lee E. Preston and Douglas P. O'Bannon "analyzes the relationship between indicators of corporate social and financial performance within a comprehensive theoretical framework". "The results, based on data for 67 large U. S. Corporations, reveal no significant negative social – financial performance relationships and strong positive correlations in both contemporaneous and lead – lag formulations" (Preston and O'Bannon, 1997). A Chinese scholar Wang Xianping wrote an article in 2006 and explained that CSR is in line with economic performance. If a company can stick to honest operation, fair competition and operation in accordance with the law, it can cut transaction cost as much as possible. Trust and good reputation won from CSR performance is a necessity for reliable expected profits in a long period. On the contrary, if companies focuses only on economic profits rather than social responsibilities, they are more likely to provide fake and counterfeit goods and evade taxation. In this way, it seems that companies have cut costs in the short term, but they will finally be abandoned by the public and fined by the government. Companies can't achieve good economic benefits and will

even encounter survival crisis. Hence, it is misunderstood that CSR performance only leads to increased costs. It will bring harm to companies in performing due responsibilities because managers will blame CSR for increasing costs and reducing profits. When considering performance goals, these managers will be reluctant to implement the strategy of CSR in the firm because short – term profit is more important for them.

(5) Misunderstanding 5: Social Audit is a new trade barrier for companies in international competition. The fulfillment of CSR has become an important part for companies to participate in competition and export in Pearl River Delta and Yangtze River Delta with many export – oriented manufacturing companies. Since 1990s, multinational companies have run their code of CSR through the chain of production in themselves and their suppliers and carried out Social Audit in importing. If companies fail in social audit, they will be unable to get orders and fail in exporting. Taking Shenzhen for an example, as early as in 1990s, multinational companies started social audit for companies in Shenzhen and audited industries expanded from toy to clothing, shoemaking and electronics. According to a survey, companies targeted at European and American markets have undergone Social Audit. About 81.05% of export enterprises, 100% clothing manufacturing and toy enterprises and 96% of other enterprises have undergone Social Audit (Zhong Xiaoshan, 2006). More recently, nearly 100% Chinese exportors will experience the challenge of Social Audit from foreign counterparties. It is clearly that Social Audit indeed imposes more restrictions on China's export trade as a new kind of "trade barrier".

Although there are barriers brought by frequent social audits from multinational companies, these barriers are in nature different from tariff and non – tariff barriers because the former is related to business ideas while the later is linked to trade policies of importing countries. Social Audit should be viewed not as a new – type of trade barrier but as a value of civilization and of sustainable development. It means that companies dealing with export business should take their social responsibilities, which is both internal need of adapting international competition rules for companies themselves and external need of abiding by laws in labor, environmental protection and consumer protection.

With this kind of misunderstanding, companies may view social audit as a trade restriction imposed by foreign countries rather than their own problems. Therefore, companies will be unable to take immediate actions to change their ideas. In fact, the perform-ance of CSR can help companies form competitive advantages in export. If a company cannot fulfill its social responsibilities in fierce international competition, it will be very hard for it to keep core competitiveness in the global market.

2. 4   Drivers for CSR fulfillment

The driving forces for CSR fulfillment are quite complicated in terms of contemporary companies. However, two basic drivers are institutional pressure and considerations on strategic interests. This paper argues that institutional pressure outweighs considerations on strategic interests in driving better CSR performance as well as business policies and actions in accordance with CSR.

2. 4. 1   Views on motivations of CSR

Considering the significance and motivation of CSR, different companies and scholars have different ideas. Some companies believe that CSR fulfillment plays a key role in finance profits and competitiveness. Carroll mentioned in 2001 that strategic CSR, also called strategic philanthropy, indicates that performing CSR is to achieving their own strategic goals. Charitable behaviors will do good to companies themselves and the society. The market will driven the development of responsible market players so if companies fulfill their social responsibilities, they will gain profits. Novak (1996) delineated a set of seven responsibilities. These are to:

Satisfy customers with goods and services of real value; earn a fair return on the funds entrusted to the corporation by its investors; create new wealth, which can accrue to non – profit institutions which own shares of publicly – held companies and help lift the poor out of poverty as their wages rise; create new jobs; defeat envy through generating upward mobility and giving people the sense that their economic conditions can improve, etc.

However, some companies just view CSR as an illusory strategic vision that has nothing to do with corporate financial targets. Others think that CSR is a non – profitable activity and just ignore it.

The truth is that to fulfill CSR has become a common strategic choice for more companies. This phenomenon is attributed to that more and more surveys have shown that the fulfillment of CSR is of strategic significance for companies growth. Husted argued in 2005 that "using real options theory, the notion of corporate social responsibility is developed as a real option and its implications for risk management. Real options theory allows for a strategic view of corporate social responsibility" (Husted, 2005). CSR, if viewed as a strategic issue, can bring benefits to companies which include better social reputation and stronger core competitiveness (Sharma and Vredenburg, 1998). Combining social activities with potential competitiveness, companies can do charity and improve competitiveness in the market (Porter and Kramer, 2002). Multinational companies, while are pursuing more profits in Chinese market, should stick to social justice and environmental protection in order to achieve sustainable development in Chinese market (World Business Council for Sustainable Development, 2005).

Many companies are still declined to perform CSR because there is no clear link between CSR and lower risks, better economic profits and sustainable development.

The aforementioned motivations are to analyze why companies should shoulder social responsibility from the perspective of internal strategic benefits. However, some scholars have different ideas. They believe it is institutional pressure rather than strategic interests that can guide companies to make decisions in line with CSR requirements (Husted and Allen, 2006).

There are some similar views in Chine's researches. *Report on Corporate Social Responsibility in China* (2006) pointed out that: Organizational guarantee and institutional construction within a company will influence the company's CSR performance; legal norms and social supervision are drivers for CSR performance; social institutional rules also play a big role in forming CSR awareness. Zhu (2012) argues that the institutional construction of CSR based on ISO26000 stanadards is very important for China to promote CSR iniatives.

In short, it is not enough to just rely on companies' initiative in forming CSR rules. Due to the lack of information disclosure measures, quantitative evaluations on voluntary and strategic CSR are still relatively unworked in China and beyond. As a result, if companies do bad in performing CSR, their operation will not be affected. If there is no mandatory requirement, it is more likely for the emergence of opportunism and negative externalities.

In current world, the research on other CSR drivers like institutional pressure beyond strategic interests is highly relevant to the building of CSR values and the fulfillment of social responsibility.

2.4.2   The analysis of institutional drivers for CSR performance

Based on empirical analysis of Mexican companies, Husted and Allen (2006) puts forward the theory of institutional pressure. They found that institutional pressure outweighs strategic interests in understanding social activities by multinational companies. Institutional pressure for companies always comes from three aspects: government regulations imperatives, influence from corporate policies and institutional structure and regular practices within institutions. The theory of institutional pressure provides a perspective to analyze reasons behind companies' laziness in performing CSR. It reminds us elements that define companies' CSR performance are government policies, laws and regulations, companies' policies, governance structure and culture.

The resource of institutional pressure can be divided into two aspects: External institutional environment and internal institutional arrangement (see Table 2 − 5). External institutional environment can be divided into government policies, legal systems, NGOs and media monitoring. Internal systems are corporate governance structure, organizational management structure and corporate culture.

Table 2 − 5   The resources of institutional pressure

External institutional environment	Internal institutional arrangement
Government policies	Corporate governance structure
Legal systems	Organizational management structure
Media monitoring	Corporate culture
NGOs	

(1) External institutional environment. Government policies cover protection of labor, environment and human rights. For example, Chinese government should introduce laws to ban or punish the phenomena like workers' wage deductions and violations of coal workers' rights. At the same time, government can also ask closure and tax increase for those high – polluted companies and issue policies that require annual CSR reports to the public. Legal systems include laws and regulations that provide protection for stakeholders. For example, rights and interests of consumers have been legally protected by *Law of the People's Republic of China on the Protection of Consumer Rights and Interests* in China. Government policies and laws and regulations are the mandatory force to move forward CSR fulfillment by companies.

CSR performance needs not only to be regulated by laws but also monitored by the media. From Enron bankruptcy to "the irrational behavior of funds" in Chinese stock's market, media have made great efforts to disclose public scandal. The media reports on companies' observance of laws and fulfillment of social responsibilities push forward the performance of CSR. The immediate and effective oversight by media on companies' mercenary behaviors can curb their ignorance of social responsibilities include financial fraud, fake products, lack of sincerity, neglect of environmental and labor protection.

NGOs are also an inseparable part of CSR campaign and have played a critical role in developing CSR (Huang Zhixiong, 2007). The World Bank defines NGOs as "private organizations that pursue activities to relieve suffering, promote the interests of the poor, protect the environment, provide basic social services or undertake community development". The reason why NGOs can be a driving force for CSR campaign lies in their initiatives, movements, standards and services. NGOs play an active and important role in major issues concerning CSR norming in industries. Around 1950s to 1960s, CSR movements were closely linked with labor movements and new conservation movements in major developed countries. Those movements together impose strong social pressure on the movement of legal transformation. Besides, NGOs influence the formulation and implementation of CSR standards. The increasing role of NGOs in CSR standards is highly linked with the "soft law". The "soft law", often contrasted with the so – called "hard law", refers to the rules that are neither strictly binding in nature nor completely lacking legal significance. In the context of international law, soft law refers to guidelines, policy declarations or codes of conduct which set standards of conduct. However, they are not directly enforceable. In terms of CSR, soft law laws and regulations made by NGOs have become a main source of its regulations. For example, SA8000 is "an auditable certification standard that encourages organizations to develop, maintain, and apply socially acceptable practices in the workplace. It was developed in 1997 by Social Accountability International, by an advisory board consisting of trade unions, NGOs, civil society organizations and companies". Although those standards and rules by NGOs are not law – binding and directly enforceable, they can also ensure effectiveness through NGOs which are thought as external monitors of CSR.

(2) Internal institutional arrangement. In terms of internal institutions, sound governance and management structures can promote CSR. The Principles of Corporate Governance launched by OECD in 1999 are intended to help policy makers evaluate and improve the legal, regulatory, and institutional framework for corporate governance, with a view to support economic efficiency, sustainable growth and financial stability. This is primarily achieved by providing shareholders, board members and executives as well as financial intermediaries and service providers with the right incentives to perform their roles within a framework of checks and balances. Scholars in favor of the stakeholder theory argue that a stakeholder as a person or group that can affect or be affected by an organization. Stakeholders can come from inside or outside of the business. Examples include customers, employees, stockholders, suppliers, non – profit groups, government, and the local community, among many others. The core idea of stakeholder theory is that organizations that manage their stakeholder relationships effectively will survive longer and perform better than organizations that don't.

Management structure within an institution can be regarded as a part of corporate governance structure. Within management structure, companies can strengthen monitoring and management on CSR through CSR committee and other departments. Now the corporate hierarchy is flattening, and more power is delegated in companies. Therefore, it is of great significance to establish specific management agencies on the implementation and coordination of CSR.

Corporate culture is also a driver for the building of CSR values. Such organizational culture refering to a unique management model with values as its center. CSR refering to companies, while maximizing profits, should protect profits of employees, consumers, suppliers and communities, which in nature is the practice of values in corporate culture. Hence, corporate values become the common basis for corporate culture and CSR. When a company is building its corporate values of responsibility, corporate culture is subsequently formulating. Sound corporate values cover harmony between self – development and ecological protection, clean, economical and safe development and so on. So if a company fosters such sound corporate values, it indeed is moving forward its performance on CSR.

2. 4. 3   Conclusion and enlightenment

Institutional pressure and strategic interests are two basic drivers for CSR fulfillment. Due to non – direct and non – immediate benefits brought by CSR fulfillment and laziness, institutional pressure, to some degree, outweighs strategic interests in formulating better CSR regulations and making better business decisions in line with CSR requirements.

In the development of China's CSR building, Chinese government should always keep a seat especially in the initial stage where government should push CSR development. Generally speaking, the theory of institutional pressure provides a good perspective for us to understand companies laziness in fulfilling CSR and a theoretical foundation for CSR building and implementation in China.

2. 5   Chapter summary

2. 5. 1   Summary of CSR definition

There is no uniform international definition of CSR. However, one thing is clear that basic elements of it should not only include shareholders, clients and staff benefits but also sustainable development, environmental protection and services for neighborhoods. The brief definition of CSR is the value and practice of a firm to balance economic benefits and social welfare.

According to therelated argument, this research believes that definition of commercial banks' CSR standards can consider the protection of benefits for all the stakeholders related with their business operations.

2. 5. 2   Summary of CSR theoretical skeleton

CSR originates from Europe and America in 18th or 19th century. In 1923, British Oliver Sheldon put forward the concept of "corporate social responsibility" formally. Contemporary CSR ideas only form and develop after the second world war and escalate tensions of industrial and labor relations.

The concept of CSR, is an evolving concept, namely evolving from classical view or pure economic view to socioeconomic view. Classical economics believes that the only social responsibility for corporate executives is to maximize profits of owners or shareholders. The socioeconomic view on CSR is that a company's executives should not only make profits but also protect and improve social welfare. In this aspect, company, more than a financial institution, has responsibilities of contributing to its community and society as well as making profits.

CSR has a long history and shifts from classical economic view to a socio – economic one. In the market economy, commercial companies have responsibilities for their stakeholders. And if companies can shoulder social responsibilities and return to their community, they will be able to improve their public image and achieve sustainable development in the long run.

2. 5. 3   Summary of CSR theoretical framework

Companies will perform their social responsibilities in the way of charitable donations but they are far beyond that. If a company with great debt and loss, it will be unrealistic to require a company to shoulder social responsibilities related to money such as establishing community orphan, high salaries and welfare for workers. But just as we have discussed before, CSR has different levels and stages. In different stages of life cycle, a company must fulfill its social responsibilities, with various focuses and differences. SA8000 surely is a globally recognized standard for CSR. Most of exporters need to get this certification to make sure their export business. But it is not the only standard for CSR. If companies focuses only on economic profits rather than social responsibilities, they are more likely to provide fake and counterfeit goods and evade taxation. In this way, it seems that companies have cut costs in the short term, but they will finally be abandoned by the public and fined by the government. Companies can't achieve good economic benefits and will even encounter survival crisis as a result. Hence, it is misunderstood that CSR performance only leads to increased costs. Although there are barriers brought by frequent social audits from multinational companies, Social Audit should be viewed not as a new – type of trade barrier but as a value of civilization and sustainable development. Therefore, the fulfillment of CSR is the process management with open ending. And different companies should have their own CSR value and code, with commercial banks no exception.

2. 5. 4 Summary of drivers for CSR fulfillment

The resource of institutional pressure can be divided into two aspects: external institutional environment and internal institutional arrangement. External institutional environment can be divided into government policies, legal systems, NGOs and media monitoring. Internal systems are corporate governance structure, organizational management structure and corporate culture. All of the above can require, guide and stimulate CSR building and fulfillment. Institutional arrangements with legal binding are the top priority.

In the development of China's CSR building, Chinese government should always keep a seat especially in the initial stage where government should push CSR development. Generally speaking, the theory of institutional pressure provides a good perspective for us to understand companies' laziness or inetia in fulfilling CSR and a theoretical foundation for CSR building and implementation in China.

Chapter 3   Underlying Reasons of Commercial Banks' Taking Social Responsibilities

This chapter aims at further discussing the importance and necessity for commercial banks to establish or carry out the value of CSR, through analyzing underlying reasons of their carrying out CSR from seven aspects.

3. 1   Introduction

For practical reasons, corporations have some intrinsic drive to undertake social responsibilities. When getting benefits from market power, companies would be willing to undertake social responsibilities, i. e., the choice of consumers is the strongest drive for companies to undertake CSR (Sen, 2003). For root reasons, including economic factors, ethical factors and legal factors, while economic factors are the most fundamentally intrinsic drive for companies' socially responsible behaviors under the condition of market economy (Ju Fanghui et al., 2005). If the public awareness becomes strong enough to transform into consumers' currency options, companies not undertaking CSR would be under the treat of market punishment, while those undertaking CSR can not only improve their corporate image, but also bring long – term benefits for themselves, thus, undertaking responsibilities gradually becomes the initiative option of modern companies.

As remarked in chapter two, for driving forces of CSR, institutional pressures can be stronger facilitation than strategic interests. As institutional arrangements, government policies, laws and regulations, media supervision and so on play key roles in developing value of CSR. For example, in many American media investigations, when asked "What kind of corporation deserves respect?" Most interviewees answer the steady profit, stable growth, safe work environment, products and services of high quality, good commercial ethics and social responsibilities. In recent years, "social responsibility" also appears in the advertising words of the TV program in CCTV economic channel. It's obvious that both mass media and government in both China and abroad are constantly strengthening the awareness of importance of undertaking CSR for modern corporations. Attentions from media and government constitute practical pressure for corporations. For improving commercial environment, corporations' actively undertaking social responsibilities is of practical significance.

Some scholars even hold that, however, for any commercial companies, including commercial banks, maximizing profit is the ultimate goal, while undertaking CSR is a means of getting expected profits in the competing environment in the future market, and also, from the angle of both corporations and shareholders, the necessity to undertake CSR can be elaborated (Lei Xongwei, 2006). From the angle of firms, first, undertaking CSR may directly or indirectly influence staff's attitude of work, contribute to the formation of good corporate culture, and thus make for improving staff's initiative, loyalty and coherence. Second, undertaking CSR is good for improving corporate image, thus, gaining social fame and word of mouth from consumers. Third, undertaking CSR, such as running business according to SA8000 international social responsibility standard, can help reduce trade barriers, successfully developing international market.

While from the angle of stakeholders, first, undertaking CSR is good for meeting staff's increasing needs, such as welfare, respect, and self – value fulfillment. Second, undertaking CSR is good for satisfying consumers' increasing awareness of safeguarding legal rights. Third, undertaking CSR is good for meeting the public's ever higher demands on protecting natural resources and environment. Fourth, undertaking CSR is good for meeting higher and higher government requests for corporations to promote employment, pay taxes according to law, and stimulate economy and social harmonious development.

As playing a key role in keeping social stability and economic sound development, compared with the general commercial corporations, commercial banks as the credit provider, to some extent, have the special identity and weight to the significance of under-taking social responsibilities. The first reason is that commercial banks' value of CSR has the "radiation effect" or "driving effect", that is, commercial banks can directly influence their clients' or other corporations' performing CSR (e. g. , promise not to in-vest in or loan to corporations polluting the environment) through green loan policies, investment philosophy, etc. The second reason is that commercial banks' performing CSR can directly or indirectly influence the whole national economic stability, for exam-ple, commercial banks' credit policy in real estate may influence the stability of proper-ty prices or consumer prices and may also trigger inflation if too many loans are offered.

However, as the lack of immediate, direct, obvious mutual relationships between the contribution of CSR mentioned above and the improvement of economic benefits, competitiveness or sustainability, commercial banks may tend to be inactive to perform CSR. However, the above reasons are still very superficial, or not deep enough. The detailed analysis of deep reasons influencing commercial banks' social responsibility is going to be presented as follows.

3. 2   Determinant of business era development

Seeing from over 200 years of history of commerce, the world's business develop-ment has experienced five basic eras, including the era of industrial revolution, the era of industrial entrepreneurs prevailing, the era of product – orientation, the era of market – orientation, and the era of relationship. Today's society has gone into the relationship era. In this era, the key strategic option for corporations to succeed has changed pro-foundly. For modern corporations, to keep maximizing profits in a long run and develo-ping sustainably, it is not enough to simply rely on comparative advantages brought by large – scale production, temporarily maximizing profits brought by product orientation and market orientation, but it should rely on establishing mutually beneficial and steady relationship in the long run with clients, suppliers, competitors and other parties in-volved or business partners (see Table 3 – 1) .

Table 3 – 1 Basic evolution history of world's business development

Starting time	Historical era	Key factors for successful business running or marketing
Late 1700s	Industrial revolution	Application of machines and large – scale production
Late 1800s	Industrial entrepreneurs prevailing	Product and service innovation, start emerging industry
Early 1900s	Product – orientation	Streamline work – flow, expand production scale, improve efficiency, and meet needs of demand – high market
1980s	Market – orientation	Emphasize brand image, customer – oriented, adapt to the changing consuming patterns, and win over the finite clients
1990s	Relationship	Emphasize mutually beneficial and cooperative relationships with clients, staff, competitors, suppliers and all social circles, through customized products and convenient services, try to establish steady relationship in the long run, thus help corporations achieve sustainable development

From Table 3 – 1, in the 1700s, the success of a commercial corporation mainly depended on whether it had purchased or used machines to achieve large – scale production. In the late 1800s, the success of corporations depended on the entrepreneurship of creating new industries or new products, for example, the emergence of such emerging industries as postal service, bank, insurance, transportation had greatly expanded chances to succeed. In the early 1900s, because of the rapid economic development and constantly expanding social needs, manufacturing enterprises generally didn't worry about sales, because their products could be undoubtedly sold out as long as they were of high quality and advanced, for example, when the semiconductor receiver was just invented, it could be sold out as soon as being produced. So, in this age, the success of the corporation mainly depended on the quality of products, the techniques of improving efficiency or increasing production through applying advanced production modes like streamlined workflow. In the second half of 1900s, because the supply exceeded the demand in the market, corporations faced fiercer competition. During the time, market – oriented or customer – oriented marketing strategies began to prevail, and the key to success was whether the product or service could satisfy customers' needs, and whether the brand image could be received by the majority of customers.

While in 1990s, the key success factors have changed again, that is, since then, the success of corporations has depended not only on the short – term maximization of profits through marketing or temporarily satisfying customers, but also the establishment of mutual benefits and cooperative relationship with all parties concerned or developing extensive strategic alliances, thus, to achieve mutual development, coordinated development and sustainable development.

Similarly, modern commercial banks should take social responsibilities, establish new partnership with clients (individuals, large enterprises, small enterprises, etc.) and make contributions to the society, thus, achieving their sustainable development and maximization of shareholders' profits in the long run.

Otherwise, in the relationship era, with the development of globalization, commercial banks have become transnational corporations one after another, thus, their scope of social responsibility is broadened, and the establishment of relationships is more complicated and diversified. Commercial banks should take broad social responsibilities in the local financial market, like obey local laws and regulations, respect cultural differences, object to racial discrimination, support local community's development project, support environmental protection projects, etc. These are the ground for commercial banks to successfully integrate into local society, build up business reputation and improve popularity. Only by doing this could commercial banks keep sustainable international competitiveness in the complex and volatile global market.

3. 3   Determinant of modern corporate nature

Modern corporate system has been the most important industry pattern. Coase (1937) once puts forward that the underlying reason of corporate existence lies in economizing transaction costs in the market, which is the reasonable explanation of corporate existence. From the angle of ownership, corporate system can be divided into three basic patterns, namely sole proprietorship, partnership and corporation.

Firstly, sole proprietorship is the simplest pattern, in which there's only one property owner, thus, it's the option for many small-sized enterprises. This simplest pattern has some obvious advantages, like easily set up and disband, but the disadvantage is that the owner directly manages the enterprise and assumes unlimited liability. Generally, because of lacking managing ability, the possibility for owners to do risky business may be small. Traditionally, state – owned enterprises or banks are similar to this in terms of institution of property rights. It has only one owner, that's the state, the agency cost or transaction cost is high, and the operational efficiency is very low.

Secondly, partnership is the kind of ownership based on two or above two owners' personal property, jointly set up and run by all owners. Apart from the advantages similar to sole proprietorship, the ownership of partnership has complementary advantages, and it is easy to operate and manage, while the disadvantages are that the owners must assume unlimited liability, and inside conflicts among owners can not be avoided as the trading goes on.

Thirdly, corporation is a kind of legal entity composed of many shareholders with the basic features. First, the ownership is separate from management, the shareholders elect board of directors, then board of directors employs top – level managers who manage daily affairs, thus, specialized management is realized, which is good for internal resources deployment. Second, the administration of the corporation is under contract and law, thus, it is placed under the effective public supervision, and such transaction costs as opportunism could be reduced. Third, because the shareholders assume limited liability, investors may avoid big risks, which is good for corporations to solve fund sources for large – scale production, and achieve the effect of economy of scale.

Corporation is becoming the general form for Chinese and foreign companies. Almost all economists admit that only modern corporate system can assure businesses' sustainable development. It is the corporation not the state that is the most important organization in this society (Xiong Jizhou, 2004). In the world today, state – owned enterprises or banks will finally become modern corporations. Take Britain for example, before 1979, the value created by state – owned enterprises accounted for 10% of GNP, but now the number has decreased to less than 1%. At present, almost all commercial banks are joint – stock banks. In a word, modern corporate system has been the basis of the ever growing corporate development. Obviously, appropriate separation between ownership and management assures the improvement of commercial banks' management and sustainability of development, thus, create necessary conditions for innovation – oriented and professional bankers.

However, as the reform of property rights advancing, commercial banks in China, especially state – owned banks may neglect taking CSR, especially when the management structure is not well enough or the corporation is poor – performed. Under such a circumstance, commercial banks must reemphasize the understanding and thinking of the importance of social responsibilities. At the bottom of the matter, the root reasons can be explained with followings.

State – owned banks' taking social responsibilities equals to state and government directives; joint – stock commercial banks' taking responsibilities equals to government directives' giving way to corporate management and determining on their own.

That is, after the reform of property right system, commercial banks in China should pay more attention to the profound significance of the issue of social responsibility, because for corporations, especially public listed firms, taking social responsibilities has been a requirement of Chinese authority, which should be published in their annual reports of CSR performance.

At present, except for joint – stock commercial banks, four major state – owned commercial banks have basically finished their shareholding reform, and all have successfully gone listed in the stock exchange market. After finishing shareholding reform, as a kind of special commercial corporations, the mature of commercial bank would change thoroughly, which means the modern corporate management system centering around the board of directors must be established within commercial banks, to assure their business should safeguard the interests of investors and all parties concerned by establishing management system and performing a package of contractual relationship (see Figure 3 – 1) .

Company law	Securities law	Labor law	Environment law
Legal system			
Shareholders	Main contractual relationship		Creditors
Owners	**Operational system of board of directors**		Customers
Employees			Suppliers
Managers	Main contractual relationship		Community
Social norms			
Religious values	Customs	Moral and ethical standards	Industry norms

Figure 3 – 1   Operational mechanism of board of directors and corporate governance

From Figure 3 – 1, business management is the operating mechanism centering around board of directors, restricted by a series of contracts and institutional arrangement, the board of directors assumes all the liabilities stipulated in contracts, i. e. , to safeguard interests of shareholders, staff, bank and institute investors, suppliers, customers, etc. All these activities are influenced and restricted by laws and regulations (company law, securities law, Labor law, Environment law, Bankruptcy law and government regulations) and social norms (religious values, customs, moral and ethical standards, industry norms), and so on. In other words, only by obeying these laws and regulations as well as codes of ethics can corporations better protect interests of all parties, and long – term interests of investors and owners. However, obeying these laws and regulations, morals and ethics actually means taking social responsibilities for all parties concerned.

For modern commercial banks, as a joint – stock company, there are no differences in nature from other commercial corporations. Their governance structure by nature determines that commercial banks must take all the responsibilities stipulated by various contracts, to safeguard interests of all parties concerned like shareholders, staff, customers, suppliers, government, communities and the general public.

3. 4　Determinant of long – term shareholder interests

More and more evidences support that corporations actively taking social responsibilities generally enjoy a higher business success rate. That's not to say that successful corporations must take more social responsibilities. Most investigations show that taking social responsibilities and achieving economic benefits are believed to be positively correlated. For example, the result of an research reveals that a firm' financial report in a short time shows that the direct expense is increasing, with the money spent on such projects as solving complaints, improving staff's welfare, environmental protection subsidizing community's service, etc. (Jeff Madura, 1998), but its economic performance in the future is indeed positively correlated with its social responsibility performance.

That's to say, it takes many years rather than a short time to test the influence of taking social responsibility on a corporation, whether positive or negative. The most influential conclusion on the relationship between taking social responsibilities and increasing finance performance is that there is not enough evidence to support that taking social responsibilities obviously reduces a corporation's long – term economic benefits (Robbins and Coulter, 2004). The financial institutions that overlook or refuse to take social responsibilities would cause serious obstacles for sustainable development in the financial sector (Zhang Changlong, 2006).

Seeing from reality, like Citibank and HSBC, these world – class banks, McDonalds and Ben & Jerry's, these famous transnational companies, as well as Haier and CNOOC, these Chinese well – known enterprises, taking social responsibilities helps these corporations improve social reputation as well as financial performance. The fact makes clear that public welfare devotion equals to good reputation which equals to long – term profit.

In recent years, some foreign scholars put forward a concept "credit bank" that corporations willing to take social responsibilities would win trust from shareholders, as the time goes, the trust would be saved like bank deposit, and in the long run, the accumulated "credit" would finally push bank to move forward long – term wealth and healthy development.

The determinant of long – term shareholders' interests is based on the expected value that the social public places on corporations. The general public expects modern corporations to take more social responsibilities, especially moral obligations. For corporations, taking social responsibilities has a kind of "conducting effect", i. e., through taking part in such activities as supporting charities, corporations can establish a tie between public welfare undertakings, corporations' image and clients' trust. If simply relying on corporations' verbal expression or advertising, such kind promotion methods, their conducting effect does little work. Because the public would doubt the intention and purpose behind the surface except they see with their own eyes. Taking social responsibilities, though, in the short run, would increase a corporation's operating cost, but seeing from the long run, its public image and social reputation would be improved (see Table 3 – 2). As public image improves, the corporation can establish a favorable external environment: improving its attraction to clients, increasing its profitability and expected value of stock, and raising stock prices.

Table 3 – 2   Six key factors for improving corporate reputation

Key factors	Examples
Emotional attraction	Respect received, consumer' trust, good impression
Products and service	Quality, innovation, reliability, customer value
Financial performance	Profitability, high expected value, low – risk investment, strong competitiveness
Leadership	Far – sighted, open – minded, ability to lead, seizing market opportunity
Work environment	Orderly management, safe workplace, staff with strong capability, good image of offices
Social responsibilities	Subsidizing charities, being responsible to environmental protection, being kind to relevant parties

Similarly, after the reform of shareholding reform, Chinese commercial banks actively taking social responsibilities are the most effective protection for shareholders' long – term interests. More specifically, to take social responsibilities, commercial banks can do the followings, for example, take responsibility in safeguarding safety in public places and protecting workers' labor, which can reduce the happening of safety crisis and casualty accidents, thus cutting down commercial banks' costs on accident indemnity and medical expenses; make contributions to fair employment, respect employee diversity and improve social welfare, which can help to increase employees' motivation, thus improving commercial banks' working efficiency and quality; take social responsibilities in clients' safety and protecting consumers' rights and interests, which can improve commercial bank's social image, strengthen customers' loyalty, thus stabilizing the client resource and relationship; take social responsibilities in obeying business ethical norms, thus strengthening commercial banks' sincerity and credit base; take social responsibilities in subsiding charities, which can improve commercial banks' popularity and influence, thus strengthening their market competitiveness. What's more, in fact, obey ethical regulations and codes of ethics is the biggest responsibility, commercial banks should take for investors, because it can fundamentally guarantee shareholders' long – term investment safety and profit maximization.

3. 5   Determinant of inclusive ecological environment

The theory of inclusive ecological environment is based on the basic principle of corporation's sustainable development. The basic principle is that in business running, a corporation should combine needs of itself with needs of relevant parties, because any corporation can not operate outside the big social environment as an independent economic entity. The significance of a corporation's business activities in the economic filed cannot be divided from the significance for society and human beings. That's to say, the goal of modern corporations should be, through combining benefits of a corporation itself, society and environment (see Table 3 – 3) and maximizing shareholders' interests as well as the relevant parties' interests, to achieve the society's and the corporation's harmonious development.

Table 3 – 3   Benefits for corporations taking social responsibilities

Corporate benefits	Social benefits	Environmental benefits
Improve financial performance	Pay tax according to law, support the national and regional construction of public facilities	Use recycling materials more frequently
Reduce operational costs	Support employees' volunteer programmes	Improve products' durability and functions
Improve image and reputation	Take part in community education, and promote personnel training	Use more renewable resources
Increase sales and improve customer loyalty	Create employment opportunities	Advocate green marketing, and sell environmentally friendly products
Respect employee diversity, and bring in new ideas on business running	Invest in public sanitation, and prevent AIDS, drug – taking	Adopt environmentally friendly modes of production, reduce pollution, and reduce diseconomies

Continued Table

Corporate benefits	Social benefits	Environmental benefits
Improve productivity and quality	Make charitable donation, and help people in need and vulnerable groups	Share good ecological and sustainable development
Reduce supervision costs	Obey commercial ethics, and establish social morality	Benefit offsprings
Bring convenience to financing	Improve social popularity, and share friendly business environment	Benefit all human beings

Both social environment and natural environment are what corporations rely on. Without a good living environment, corporations can not live sustainably. So, it can be said that social benefits and environmental benefits are also the parts of corporations' benefits. Overlooking any one of them may cause the lose of ecological based on which sustainable development and prosperity rely. From this aspect, corporations actively taking social responsibilities are creating a good ecological environment for themselves. This ecological environment is the foundation of corporate sustainable development.

To establish a harmoniously ecological base for corporations' sustainable development is one of the greatest concepts in the 21st century. Just as mentioned above, the birth and development of the concept of modern corporate social responsibility, is closely related to the evolution of the thinking, environmental protection and sustainable development, while the birth of the concept of sustainable development is directly related to the increasing serious environment pollution. In 1987, World Commission on Environment and Development released the Brundtland Report, and made a systematic explanation on the concept of sustainable development, and summarized the concept as three key elements: environmental protection, economic development and social equity, i. e. , to achieve ecological sustainability, economic sustainability and social sustainability. These three elements are broadly consistent with the three kinds of benefits (see Table 3 - 3) driving modern corporations to take social responsibilities. More specifically, ecological sustainability is environmental benefit, which is the natural base for corporations' sustainable development; economic sustainability is economic benefit, which is the material source for corporations to achieve the long – term maximization of profits;

social sustainability is social benefit, which refers to the sustainable development in other aspects except for ecology and economy, for example, pay attention to effective control on reproduction and life quality, thus to eliminate the unequal distribution of wealth
and effective management of interests. Only in a social environment where people's
equality, freedom and human rights can be guaranteed can corporations' living environment develop soundly, and achieve sustainable development in the real sense.

To some extent, commercial banks' social responsibility can be described as
"commercial banks' contribution to the sustainable development of society". In other
words, sustainable development is a vital part of commercial banks' social responsibilities. This is determined by commercial banks' special position and function in economy, society and environment. On the one hand, the cause of environmental problem is
mainly related to commercial banks' credit policies and management behaviors, which
is the result of "external diseconomy". On the other hand, although commercial banks
are not the only force to push sustainable development, yet whether for their own development or whole society's development, their solution plays an important role in social or
economic development. For commercial banks, as the important cell of the whole society, only by promoting economic, social and environmental sustainable development can
they themselves achieve sustainable development. If disregarding environmental benefits
and social benefits, simply pursuing short – term economic benefits, like providing loans
to polluting enterprises, sooner or later, commercial banks would get punishment from
nature or society. In this sense, under a harmonious environment, commercial banks'
contributions to social sustainability can be regarded as devoting to their own sustainable
development.

3.6   Determinant of regulatory constraints

According to this point of view, all corporations must take social responsibilities because of constraints from government's regulations, like *Antimonopoly Law* and *Company
Law* protecting fair competition, *Consumer Rights Protection Act* and *Product Safety Law*
protecting consumers' rights and interests, *Labor Law* and *Fair Employment Regula-*

tions, *Social Insurance Laws and Regulations*, *Model Business Principles* and *Protection Law for the Disabled* protecting employees' safety and interests, *Environmental Protection Law* protecting environment from being polluted. These regulations constrain corporations' operational behavior, and impel corporations to actively take responsibilities. However, to a large extent, the concept of social responsibilities in legal aspect is only one aspect, which does not include other social responsibilities, such as ethical aspects and voluntary aspects, but in fact, corporate social responsibilities more refer to these non – mandatory duties. Social responsibilities stipulated by laws and regulations are mandatory, corporations must obey unconditionally, otherwise, it would be regarded as illegal, and thus assume legal responsibilities. Social responsibilities stipulated by laws and regulations are a part of social responsibilities which corporations should take, and the binding force is confined only to this aspect, not binding for other social responsibilities.

What needs to be specifically proposed is that generally corporations' taking social responsibilities is regarded to be voluntary and non – mandatory, but this is not to say that corporations can treat these social responsibilities at will and these social responsibilities have nothing to do with mandatory legal duties. Because on the one hand, there exists a strong external supervision and market pressure, if the corporation can't perform moral and voluntary social responsibilities, it will face public opinion, moral condemnation and boycott from consumers union, etc. , which may directly influence corporate social image, thus directly or indirectly influencing corporate economic performance, and this is an invisible constraint for corporations. On the other hand, behaviors related to social responsibilities like prohibiting child labor, protecting environment, protecting labor and employees' welfare, etc. have been, more or less, stipulated in *Labor Law*, *Environmental Protection Law*, etc. , thus becoming their legal obligations. In some degrees, the rise of the concept of corporate social responsibilities is the correcting or making up for incomplete government regulations, while after these social responsibilities become social consensus, they tend to be confirmed by law, thus becoming mandatory legal responsibilities.

Similar with any other commercial corporations, commercial banks' taking social responsibilities is restricted subject to relevant regulations. Apart from above legal constraints, there exist many financial laws and regulations regulating their behaviors, such as *Law of Commercial Bank*, *Anti - money Laundering Regulations*, *Foreign Exchange Laws*, *Equator Principle* and *Green Credit Rules* etc. For example, under the Article 8 of *Commercial Banking Law of the People's Republic of China*, commercial banks must run business in accordance with the laws and relevant administrative regulations, and they shall not impair the national and public interests. This regulation doesn't cover the overall and specific requirement for commercial banks' taking social responsibilities, but the regulation itself would suggest that commercial banks should take important social responsibilities for the national construction and social development.

3. 7   Determinant of social contract

Social contract determinant is similar with the determinant of nature of modern corporations. The theory holds to a more broader social contract which surpasses the law and believes that the base of corporate functions is the social contract. As a member of a society, given the right to exist and operate, corporations are supposed to take social responsibilities, that is in any case, they should actively adapt to the change of social expectations, and flexibly make responses to social responsibilities. Under the social contract, there exists a lower limit for corporate social responsibilities, but it is hard to make a upper limit. The lower limit is that corporations are responsible to take economic and legal responsibilities, while upper limit extends to moral responsibilities, of which the concept is unconstrained.

What's more, under the social contract, corporations are the sum of relationship between corporations and the society. The contractual relationship between corporations and relevant parties is very complicated, and the corporations is responsible to achieve a balance between corporate and social contractual relationships, i. e. , make contributions to the improvement of society and economy. As a small group, corporations must accept the management of big group, that is the government. Although the government has the unshakable responsibilities for social development and the public, since corporations operate under the existent laws and social regulations, they should actively cooperate with the government in order to achieve more extensive social objectives.

3. 8   Determinant of globalization

Since 1990s, as the advancement of globalization and trade liberalization, the campaign of social responsibility spreads to the international world, and has developed rapidly and swept across the whole world at the turn of the century. In recent years, our country has been enjoying the convenience since joining WTO, but at the same time, suffering the pain of anti – dumping and technology barrier. Some Chinese corporations, for example, Wenzhou Leather Shoes Enterprise had its foreign store in Spain burned by the local customer; more and more export enterprises are facing the challenge of social audit from American and European countries' importers. Under the globalization, the campaign of social responsibilities continues to flourish, as the strong pressure, drives Chinese corporations to pay attention to social responsibilities, that is, that modern corporations actively taking social responsibilities are under the background of globalization and have distinctive features. More specifically, the background of globalization includes changes in international politics, economies, technologies and social environment. For example, because of joining WTO, the communication between governments has been expanded, the cooperation in human rights, labor, and environmental protection is strengthened; for economy, the rapid development of transnational enterprises has linked the world together, but it has also brought attention to the local environmental protection and labor protection; for technology, the adoption of such technologies as information, transportation and communication technologies has facilitated communication and trade, but has also brought problems like the protection of intellectual property rights; for social changes, like the increase of cultural diversity among employees and transnational marriages, has brought the issue of respecting and recognizing the multicultural employees. All these changes resulting from globalization have helped to expand the scope of social responsibilities that modern corporations should take, and the necessity of establishing core values of social responsibilities. Therefore, earnestly fulfilling social responsibilities is being strengthened. In other words, it is under the background of globalization that the concept of corporate social responsibility has become increasingly complicated and important, and has obtained more and more attention.

The internationalization of commercial banks is advancing rapidly, so global operations of banks will be imperative. During participating in global operations, taking social responsibilities is regarded as core competitiveness by more and more commercial banks. Social Audit has been becoming the barrier or threshold of market access for commercial banks. If failing to operate in accordance with international convention, local regulations and cultural customs, commercial banks undoubtedly can't live and develop in the host country. From this point of view, globalization determines that commercial banks must take much broader social responsibilities in global market, but seeing from a strategic height and long – term interest, they should regard the maximization of social responsibility as one of their most important management goals and core values.

Chapter 4　Empirical Research on Commercial Banks' CSR

This chapter aims at identifying reasons why commercial banks should take CSR through case studies, analyzing the weakness in taking CSR of Chinese commercial banks and suggestions to improve, with reference to foreign commercial banks' performance and questionnaire survey, thus to further explain the necessity of taking CSR of Chinese commercial banks, and offer suggestions for establishing a measuring standard and mechanism.

4. 1　Practices of well – known foreign banks' taking CSR

Under the background of globalization, the scope of commercial banks' CSR becomes increasingly broad to include fair employment, supply – chain management, community investment, voluntary service, environmental protection, sustainable financing, etc. Generally speaking, more and more foreign commercial banks concern about CSR, actively establish relevant management mechanism, and make contributions to society. In addition, it is proved that the more popular a bank is, the more contribution it makes to society.

Traditionally, for some foreign commercial banks, it has relied on actively taking CSR to ensure corporate sustainable prosperity and development, for example, the founder of JP Morgan, the so – called "century – long shop" in the financial circle, has said that the key for its lasting prosperity lies in sincere and responsible management concept, rather than manipulating financial market, making unethical gains, and threatening the stability of society and economy under the market – oriented economy. This concept itself suggests a kind of social responsibility.

CSR has obtained a widespread concern among western commercial banks. Most of them have taken effective measures to strengthen relevant work. For example, more and more foreign commercial banks have integrated CSR into their strategic goals, joined in international CSR organization to regulate business running, operated according to international SR standards, and published their annual SR reports. In recent years, some foreign commercial banks' performance on taking social responsibilities can be seen from Table 4 – 1.

Table 4 – 1　World famous banks' performance on taking CSR

Bank name	CSR activities
Barclays	Promote sustainable financing and community investment
Standard chartered	Support AIDS prevention and rehabilitation
HSBC	Reduce hydrogen peroxide and air pollution emission, and support the cause of environmental protection
Citibank	Implement credit policy protecting forests and reducing pollution
Bank of America	Improve employee's welfare, care about single – parent families and life needs of workers from minority areas
Wachvia	Increase investment, subsidize low – income families housing and community infrastructure construction
ABN AMRO	Actively establish shareholder protection principle, and apply sustainable development standards into business activities
HSBC	Establish charitable institution, support voluntary work and school education projects in local communities

Some well – known commercial banks in foreign countries actively join in the international CSR organization, and consciously regulate business activities according to the guidelines. Joining in international CSR organization has been a trend followed by international large banks. For example, on June 4ᵗʰ, 2003, in Washington, ten large banks from seven countries declared to accept "Equator Principles" (a set of principles on social and environmental protection relevant to develop and manage project financing) .

The Equator Principles is a risk management framework, adopted by financial institutions, for determining, assessing and managing environmental and social risk in project finance. It is primarily intended to provide a minimum standard for due diligence to support responsible risk decision – making. On June 4th, 2013, 79 adopting financial institutions in 35 countries have officially adopted the Equator Principles, covering over 70 percent of international Project Finance debt in emerging markets. The Equator Principles, formally launched in Washington DC on June 4th, 2003, were based on existing environmental and social policy frameworks established by the International Finance Corporation.

The number of commercial banks implementing the principles has been increasing to include such large international banks as Barclays, HSBC, Bank of America, Wachvia, ABN AMRO, etc. These principles are based on environmental protection guidelines set by WB and IMF. Banks adopting the principles can only offer loans to environmentally – friendly projects. These banks apply these principles to almost all loan projects like mining, oil and gas industry. According to the principles, the borrower can get loans only after passing through relevant environmental assessment. The relevant assessment standards include: sustainable development, the application of renewable resources; human health, cultural heritage and biodiversity protection; the use of hazardous materials and major disasters prevention; occupation health and safety; fire and life safety; social and economic effect; land exploration; community influence; project design, testing and involvement of implementation personnel; production efficiency and energy utilization; polluting prevention and waste minimization, etc.

To sum up, from the current situation, many developed countries have attached great importance to such issues related to CSR as strategic management, business running, mechanism arrangement, management mechanism, information transparency, etc., and have taken specific and feasible commercial measures. Take HSBC as an example.

Hong Kong and Shanghai Banking Corporation (hereinafter refers to as HSBC) is the world's largest bank and one of the largest financial service institutions, established in Hong Kong since more than 140 years ago. Now, HSBC has about 9700 offices in 77 businesses. It takes local markets as sources of funds and target market, also, adopts advanced technologies to improve efficiency, and thus provides products and services accommodating to local customers.

Since 1865, HSBC has been taking CSR as its corporate basic value. All business offerings of HSBC are based on credit and fame, and the bank strives to apply the highest standards of conduct into practice. HSBC has also taken responsibilities of improving social environment of local community, bringing a better life for customers, shareholders and employees.

Based on the reports of HSBC published in recent years, the bank has some obvious changes in its practices of CSR reports, which are seen as follows: HSBC published its Sustainability Report in 2012 and 2013. But in 2014 and 2015, the bank published its Strategic Report with key facts at a glance including Communication on Progress to UN Principles for Responsible Investment, Communication on Progress to UN Principles for Sustainable Insurance, Communication on Progress to UN Global Compact, Reporting Guidelines—Equator Principles, Reporting Guidelines—Carbon Emissions. Clearly, the bank has been more specific and detailed in its transparency practices based on the CSR guidelines of UN Global Compact and Equator Principles.

Seeing from the above analysis, taking CSR through cultivating citizenship has become a common strategic option for well – known foreign commercial banks, and also, these banks have obtained great economic achievements and social fame. Thus, learning their advanced experiences and strengthening the concept of taking CSR for Chinese commercial banks are of great significance. Taking CSR would benefit social mass as well as commercial banks themselves. Commercial banks without taking "CSR" will not be able to develop sustainably. Taking CSR can help commercial banks obtain social reputation, and safeguard interests of investors and the public.

4. 2　Current situation of Chinese commercial banks' taking CSR

4. 2. 1　Current situation of Chinese financial institutions

The present Chinese commercial banks are the banks except the Central Bank (the

People's Bank of China) and the three policy banks (National Development Bank, China Import and Export Bank, Agricultural Bank of China) including four big state – owned commercial banks (Industrial and Commercial Bank of China, Agricultural Bank of China, China Construction Bank, Bank of China) and a small state – owned bank (China Postal Savings Bank), a dozen of comparatively large joint – equity commercial banks (Bank of Communications, China Merchants Bank, CITIC Industrial Bank, China Everbright Bank, Shanghai Pudong Development Bank, Hengfeng Bank and China Zheshang Bank, etc.) and many other types of commercial banks (such as city commercial banks, rural commercial banks, joint venture banks, banks with foreign capital, private banks) (see Table 4 – 2). The four big stated – owned commercial banks have made great achievements in joint – stock system reform, and finished the reform of commercialization and gone public. The financial situation of these banks has been improved significantly, and their main economic indicators come close to international large banks', and modern corporate governance mechanism has begun to play its role. Other commercial banks or financial institutions have also made great progress in reform and development.

Table 4 – 2   A list of Chinese financial institutions

Type	Number	Notes
Central bank	1	People's Bank of China
Policy banks	3	National Development Bank, China Import and Export Bank, Agricultural Bank of China
State – owned commercial banks	5	Industrial and Commercial Bank of China, Agricultural Bank of China, China Construction Bank, Bank of China, China Postal Savings Bank
Joint – stock commercial banks	12	Bank of Communications, China Merchants Bank, CITIC Industrial Bank, China Everbright Bank, Shanghai Pudong Development Bank, Hengfeng Bank and China Zheshang Bank, Guangdong Development Bank, etc.
City commercial banks and others	Over 800	Beijing City Commercial Bank, Shanghai City Commercial Bank, Guangzhou City Commercial Bank, etc.
Financial leasing firms	40	–

Continued Table

Type	Number	Notes
Public funds firms	91	—
Financial companies	115	—
Trust investment companies	68	—
Securities firms	111	—
Financing firms	265	—
Funds subsidiaries	67	—

Note: Adapted based on the website information of 2016.

The process of modernizing China's payment system has made great progress. China has basically established an extensive, trans – market and trans – regional paying system with complete services, with RMB realizing clearing arrangement in many counties and regions. The electronic trading system based on the Internet has been improved a lot, which can provide investors and consumers with the safe, efficient and convenient capital transaction and settlement services. The Central Bank has established a set of financial information monitoring system, account management, credit management, treasury management, anti – money laundering analysis, financial statistic monitoring and management, and office affairs, etc. The services like operating processing integrated, money exchange, bank card and so on, have realized computer network processing and centralized processing. In addition, new financial services like self – help bank, e – commerce, online payment and settlement are developing rapidly.

In order to accommodate the stable development of banking business under the open economy, on December 27th, 2003, the sixth session of the Standing Committee of the tenth National People's Congress passed the amendment of *Law of the People's Bank of China* and *Law of the People's Republic of China on Commercial Banks*, at the same time, *Security Law*, *Insurance Law*, *Negotiable Instrument Law*, *Trust Law* and *Law of Security Investment Fund Law* were made, relevant laws like *Bankruptcy Law* are being drafted and revised. In addition, given international convention, combining national conditions, the Central Bank and financial supervision department have carried out standards of prudent supervision, and made a series of departmental rules and regulations and guiding document, providing legal and institutional protection for financial reform, opening – up and development.

On the whole, with financial regulations and policies constantly adjusting, China's financial market will continue to improve with the application of online banking technology and ecommerce platforms, market competition mechanism will gradually be established, and commercial banks are moving towards commercialization, modernization and internationalization. We can say that the financial market of China is developing rapidly, and its future is promising.

4.2.2 Chinese commercial banks' general CSR performance

Though China's financial institutions are being perfected, and commercial banks are developing soundly, there are still some obvious problems in commercial banks' performance of taking CSR, which cannot be overlooked. More specifically, the major problems are as follows:

(1) Lack of annual CSR report system. Based on our survey, there are just quite few commercial banks in China which have announced their annual CSR reports to the public, showing that on both the strategic level, and the operational level, Chinese commercial banks do not have a clearly – defined position of CSR management and a sufficient awareness of the problem in their institutional arrangement.

(2) Insufficient participation in the Equator Principle. So far as we research, currently, there are quite few Chinese commercial banks that have joined the Equator Principle, a voluntary code for environmentally responsible project financing by commercial and investment banks, to automatically regulate their investment on projects based on the environment – friendly principle or the so – called green lending policy. In November. 2008, China's Industrial Bank decided to join in the Equator Principle, as an unrealized exception. In general, the lack of participation of Chinese commercial banks in the Equator Principle shows that the Chinese commercial banks have not recognized the importance of this principle and CSR performance.

(3) Loosened control of lending activities. The lending policies of some commercial banks are not socially responsible, for example, some banks disregard the government's green credit move and still offer funds to those businesses which belong to high –

pollution industry in order to boost profits; some banks invest heavily and blindly in individual real estate markets which lead to the increasing prices of property or even financial crisis; few banks would like to willingly support the national policy of solving SMEs financing problems to offer loans to SMEs although they need funds urgently, etc.

(4) Some involvement of unfair treatment. Some state – owned commercial banks still set barriers to market entry, some cooperate under the table with securities to earn profits through black arrangement, and some provide commission or to customers so as to take in business through bribery, which may destroy the principle of fair competition in the financial market.

(5) Not strictly sticking to the principle of trust and honesty. Some commercial banks in recent years have been criticized by the public and media for their nontransparent charging of electronic withdrawing and transferring services to customers, for example, the World Economy of Economist. ICXO. com reports that experts criticize the nontransparent pricing of commercial banking card services as aggressive pricing strategy.

(6) Insufficient support to charitable causes. Some commercial banks do not actively participate in the donation to social causes. Based on based Huyun Charity Donation Ranking Enterprises 2005, among the top ten donators, there is only one bank in the list which is a foreign bank. In 2007, among the top ten donators, there are two banks which are HSBC and Bank of Communications. Similarly in 2014, there is only one bank on the top 30 enterprise donators' ranking order, which is Minsheng Bank. However, the highest – ranking firms in the Fortune 500 based on their total assets such as ICBC, ABC, BOC and CCB are all in the list, showing that, to some extent, their social donation and their financial strengths are not balanced in their business operations.

(7) Giving little consideration to social employment issue. China is in the period of industrial structuring, so many industries including banks are cutting off employees. In the process of reforming, some banks, on the excuse of downsizing for efficiency, laid off a large number of employees. This may be a necessary choice for commercialized operation, but laying off employees disregarding all consequences is irresponsible.

(8) Breaking the fair competition principle. Some commercial banks lack the sense of fair competition, especially those banks dominating market try to control finan-

cial market, continue to make monopoly profits, and destroy competition. Some commercial banks and security enterprises attempt to manipulate stock market, control information transparency, and make illegal profit. Some banks use disreputable methods like rebate, entertaining clients to solicit business, which break the fair competition principle and market environment.

In summary, these facts indicate that Chinese commercial banks are now facing the challenges of how to be more socially responsible in their business operations, not saying how to take the lead in implementing socially responsible and sustainable development concepts and strategies. Analyzing the specific factors causing these issues may contribute to take proper actions to solve the problems.

4.2.3   Factors causing the CSR problems

First, related laws and regulations.

In the Western developed nations, a majority of them have redefined their company law to include the contents of CSR in their provisions, so as to protect the interests of related stakeholders such as owners, customers, employees and local communities. However, in the *Company Law of the People's Republic of China* issued in 1995 and amended recently, such as Article 4: The shareholders of a company shall enjoy such rights as benefiting from assets of the company, making major decisions and selecting managerial personnel in accordance with the law; and Article 17: Companies must protect the lawful rights and interests of their staff and workers, sign labor contracts with them and cover them with social insurances in accordance with the law, and strengthen labor protection so as to achieve safety in production. It just specifies the protection of the interests of investors and employees, but other stakeholders such as local communities and the general public are not clearly specified. Such an ignorance of CSR may be one of the reasons for the CSR problems of Chinese commercial banks.

Second, economic institutional transmission.

State – owned enterprises are more likely to undertake more social responsibilities as the requirement of government while privatized ones may be not so. However, Chinese stated – owned commercial banks have been more and more privatized as a result of share ownership reform in recent years. Along with privatization and commercialization, these commercial banks may not undertake social responsibilities as required by the government, but they may undertake fewer social responsibilities according to their own willingness and strength. In addition, in the evaluation of excellence, the government authority or media has overvalued the economic performance of a business or bank, and has attached less attention to the social contribution, which inevitably weakens the emphasis of commercial banks on their contribution to CSR programs.

Third, corporate cultural issues.

Corporate culture is regarded as the value direction of a successful business. Modern commercial banks, as a special profit – seeking business providing financial services, should also establish a good corporate culture of corporate social responsibilities such as balancing social effects and economic benefits in managerial decisions and operations, so as to maintain sustainable development. However, Chinese commercial banks, especially the state – owned commercial banks, took social responsibilities in the past out of the mandatory orders of the government, which means there was no establishment of commercial business culture. After being suddenly reformed into commercial banks responsible for taking their own risks in the real sense, they have not established commercial business culture, but tended to consider the maximization of profits as the center of decision – making, and may incorrectly consider their contribution to social causes which will only increase costs with no direct profits.

Forth, corporate governance.

Corporate governance has been one of the widely – studied topics in the past 20 years. It is defined as a set of systems to check and balance the influences and interests of all interest groups of a business such as investors, managers, employees, customers, and local communities, etc. The relationship of checking and balancing different stakeholders is realized through the internal institutional arrangement of board of directors, committee of supervision and level of management as well as through the external institutional arrangement of laws and regulations in the related markets.

In China, commercial banks, particularly the state – owned commercial banks, are commonly imperfect in corporate governance after their recent years' reformation of stock ownership, for example, firstly, as a result of board director usually as party secretary being heavily involved in the daily management of human resources, CEO may lose some control of human resources management; as a result of CEO appointed by the government authority, he, as the manager of daily banking operations, may pursue the short – term attainment of goals or short – term profit rather than long – term sustainable development; as a result of lack of external independent directors in supervision committee, the directors cannot fully play their role of supervision. In summary, in shortage of efficient internal supervision, the mangers of commercial banks may naturally ignore the interests of other stakeholders.

4. 3   Questionnaire and data analysis of banks' CSR performance

4. 3. 1   Questionnaire studies and analysis

(1) Aim and method of the study. The aim of this case study are to further testify three aspects aforementioned: first, to testify how employees in China commercial banks know about CSR, especially the definition and importance; second, to testify defects of CSR management system in Chinese commercial banks; third, to testify problems in specific activities for China commercial banks taking CSR. In addition, it will propose some suggestions on setting CSR standards and mechanisms.

This study is conducted in the way of questionnaire, with the content including 15 related issues (see Appendix 1), such as the reorganization of concept and importance of CSR (relationship between relevant standards, types and company's image and sustainable development etc.), company's CSR management system (management body, annual report, etc.), specific activities for companies taking CSR (protect employees' interests, environmental awareness, volunteer labor, safeguard social and national economy etc.) . The design of this questionnaire refers to the relevant reports by Chinese CSR development center and CSR evaluation system, combining with the specific situation. The author designed and made some revises, like deleting child labor issue and adding something with commercial banks' characteristics, like supporting state's macro – economic security policy, taking clients' environmental awareness into consideration when granting loans, thus to highlight the distinctiveness of the issue.

The objects of this survey are mainly commercial banks, including joint – stock commercial banks and state – owned commercial banks. The major ways are visiting, asking and filling out. The author personally visited or sent college students to visit 12 commercial banks in China, directly gave questionnaires to work stuff in commercial banks or indirectly through emails. Totally about 220 questionnaires were sent out, and 160 valid questionnaires were received. During the process, most interviewees were co-operative, thanks to their support and cooperation.

(2) Analysis of the results.

1) Have you heard of the following concepts of CSR in working or receiving train-ings in your bank?

A. Corporate social responsibility　　　　B. SA8000

C. Equator principle　　　　　　　　　　D. Not sure

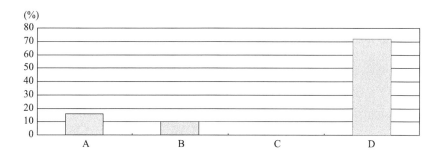

Figure 4 – 1　Answers to question 1

Results show that (see Figure 4 – 1), 16% interviewees have received CSR con-cept during working and training, 10% have heard SA8000, have heard "Equator Prin-ciple", while 72% don't know CSR. This suggests that commercial banks' attention on CSR and relevant propaganda are not enough, which cause employees' knowing little a-bout CSR.

2) Does your bank record CSR activities and release reports on CSR?

A. Often　　　　　B. Occasionally　　　　　C. Never

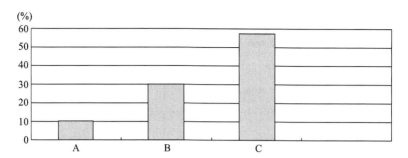

Figure 4 – 2   Answers to question 2

Results are that (see Figure 4 – 2), 10% interviewees chose A, 30% chose B, while 57% chose C. This suggests that nearly 60% Chinese commercial banks does nothing on CSR management or reporting.

3) Does your bank set up the following management departments?

A. Social responsibility department

B. Sustainable development department

C. Public relation department

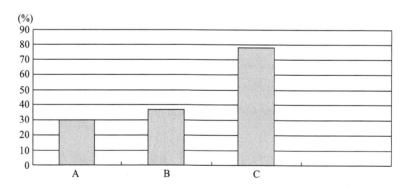

Figure 4 – 3   Answers to question 3

Results show that (see Figure 4 – 3) 30% interviewees answer there's a social responsibility department in their bank, 37% answer there's a sustainable development department in their bank, and over 78% answer that there's a public relation department in their bank. This suggests that most China commercial banks haven't set up a specialized CSR management department, i. e. , the management level hasn't taken CSR seriously.

4) Will your bank take clients' environmental protection into consideration when granting loans?

A. Yes   B. No   C. Not sure

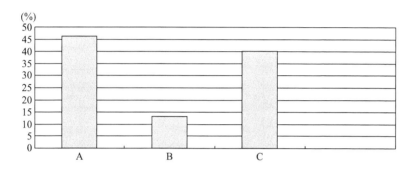

Figure 4 – 4   Answers to question 4

Results are that (see Figure 4 – 4) 46% chose A, 13% chose B, and 40% chose C. This suggests that China commercial banks' environmental awareness is improving, the concept of green investment is strengthening, while still over half of the banks don't consider or not always consider CSR issue in granting loans.

5) Does your bank participate in any public welfare activities or donations?

A. Often   B. Yes   C. No

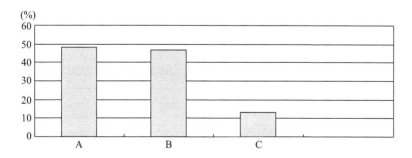

Figure 4 – 5   Answers to question 5

Results are that (see Figure 4 – 5) 48% chose A, 47% chose B, and 13% chose C. This suggests that more and more Chinese commercial banks participate in public affairs, and most of them have participated in donations.

6) Has your bank bought social insurance and medical insurance for you and pay overtime wages?

A. Yes, for all staff   B. Yes, but not all   C. No

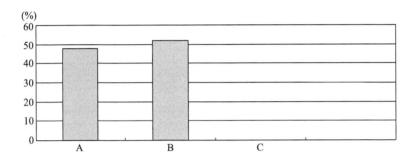

Figure 4 – 6   Answers to question 6

Results are that (See Figure 4 – 6) 48% chose A, 52% chose B, and no one chose C. This suggests that Chinese commercial banks generally perform well in employee welfare treatment.

7) Does your bank pay salary or subsidy on time?

A. Often   B. Occasionally   C. Never

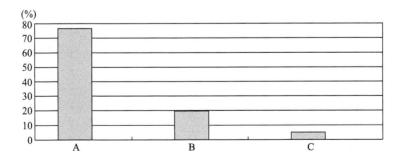

Figure 4 – 7   Answers to question 7

Results are that (see Figure 4 – 7) 76% chose A, 19% chose B, and 5% chose C. Similar with last question, this suggests that most Chinese commercial banks generally perform well in employee welfare treatment.

8) Does gender age discrimination exist in your bank?

A. Yes   B. No

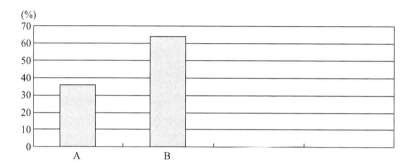

Figure 4 – 8   Answers to question 8

Results are that (see Figure 4 – 8) 36% chose A, and 64% chose B. This suggests that comparatively serious sexism and ageism exist in China commercial banks and these commercial banks do not perform very well on CSR in terms of employment.

9) Do nontransparent or unreasonable charges exist in your bank?

A. Often   B. Occasionally   C. Never

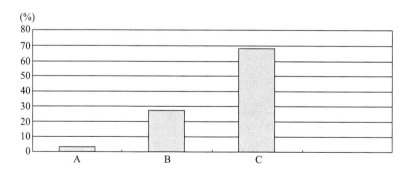

Figure 4 – 9   Answers to question 9

Results are that (see Figure 4 −9) 3% chose A, 27% chose B, and 68% chose C. This suggests, as a whole, most Chinese commercial banks perform well in protecting consumers' right to know, but still 30% interviewees admit that their banks have often or occasionally conducted nontransparent or unreasonable charges, and some problems in taking CSR which cannot be neglected do exist in China commercial banks. This also conforms with the frequent report on issues of nontransparent charges.

10) Have you taken state's macro economic policy and local development policy into consideration when you are working?

A. Yes   B. Occasionally   C. Never

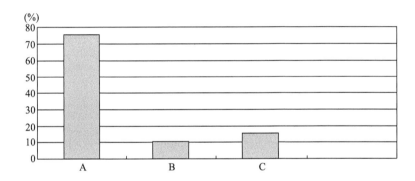

Figure 4 – 10   Answers to question 10

Results are that (see Figure 4 − 10) 75% chose A, 10% chose B, and 15% chose C. This suggests that most commercial banks consciously carry out and support state's macro − economic policy and local development policy, i. e. , bear high sense of CSR. While still 25% believe that commercial banks never or occasionally carry out and support state's macro − economic policy and local development policy i. e. misunderstandings towards CSR still exist in some commercial banks. In fact, commercial banks play an important role in economic sustainability and social stability.

11) What do you think social responsibilities of commercial banks should include?

A. Economic responsibility   B. Legal responsibility

C. Ethic responsibility   D. Voluntary philanthropic responsibility

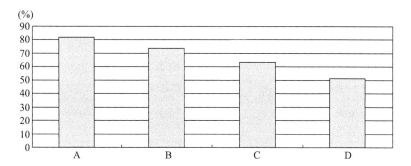

Figure 4 – 11　Answers to question 11

Above four options are all CSRs that commercial banks should take. While the Results are that (see Figure 4 – 11) 82% chose A, 73% chose B, 63% chose C, and 51% chose D. This suggests that generally speaking, Chinese commercial banks and bank staff begun to realize the basic meaning of CSR, that is to say, banks should not simply pursue economic interests but also should obey laws and ethics, and support charitable undertakings. However, bank staff still put economic interests first, emphasize the philosophy that all should serve the maximization of economic benefits, which goes against with the concept of corporate social responsibility.

12) What do you think commercial banks' CSR should be seen as?

A. Paying taxes honestly　　　　　B. Commercial ethics

C. Shareholders' interests　　　　　D. Public welfare undertakings

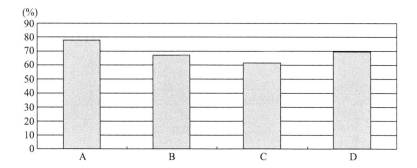

Figure 4 – 12　Answers to question 12

Above four options are all contributions commercial banks should make. While the Results are that (see Figure 4 – 12) 78% chose A, 67% chose B, 61% chose C, and

70% chose D. Interviewees' choices are well – distributed, which suggests that bank staff's awareness of CSR is increasing.

13) What do you think taking CSR will bring to banks ?

A. Financial burden   B. Cost reduce

C. Long – term interest   D. Efficiency improvement

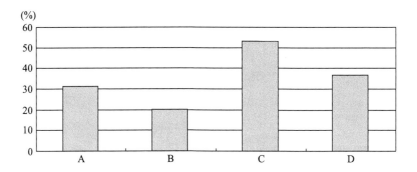

Figure 4 – 13   Answers to question 13

The Results are that (see Figure 4 – 13) 31% chose A, 20% chose B, 53% chose C, and 37% chose D. This suggests that most of the bank staff believe that taking CSR can bring banks' long – term benefits, which lays a good mass base for commercial banks' taking CSR.

14) Do you think taking CSR have anything to do with bank's sustainable development?

A. Yes   B. No   C. Not sure

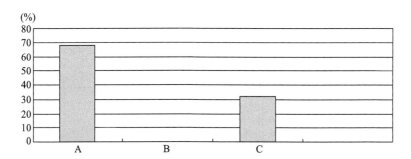

Figure 4 – 14   Answers to question 14

The Results are that (see Figure 4 – 14) 68% chose A, no one chose B, and 32% chose C. This suggests that most bank staff believe that taking CSR is closely related to bank's sustainable development, which reflects the importance and necessity of commercial banks taking CSR, and the good mass foundation for Banks' taking CSR in expectation.

15) Do you think taking CSR means a lot to bank's image?

A. Very important　　　　B. Important　　　　C. Not so much

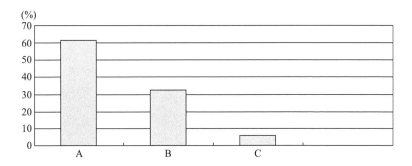

Figure 4 – 15　Answers to question 15

The Results are that (see Figure 4 – 15) 62% chose A, 32% chose B, and 6% chose C. This suggests that over 90% bank staff think taking CSR means a lot to the increase of bank's image, which reflects the importance and necessity of commercial banks' taking CSR, and the good mass base for commercial banks to take CSR.

(3) Comparative analysis with studies on other firms. According to categories of CSR, the 15 questions can be divided into 3 types: first, commercial banks' recognition of importance of taking CSR, like Q11, Q12, Q13, Q14 and Q15; second, commercial banks' CSR management mechanism, like Q1, Q2 and Q3; third, commercial banks' CSR practices, like Q4 and Q10. In addition, according to the protection of shareholders' interests, the above questions can also be divided into 3 types: first, protect employees' interests, like Q6, Q7 and Q8; second, protect clients' interests like Q9; third, protect community and public's interests, like Q4, Q5 and Q10. What should be emphasized is that Q5 and Q10 are additional questions, scholars like Ying

Gefei of Chinese CSR development center didn't mention these questions in their questionnaires, thus there's no relevant data to compare (see Table 4 – 3).

Table 4 – 3   Comparative data of commercial banks and other firms' CSR

Part 1 Data sheet of questionnaire on Chinese commercial banks' CSR (%)			
Question number	Option A	Option B	Option C	Option D
Q1	16	10	0.1	72
Q2	10	30	57	—
Q3	30	37	78	—
Q4	46	13	40	—
Q5	48	47	3	—
Q6	48	52	0	—
Q7	76	18	15	—
Q8	36	64	—	—
Q9	3	27	68	—
Q10	75	10	15	—
Q11	82	73	68	51
Q12	78	67	61	70
Q13	31	20	53	37
Q14	68	68	32	—
Q15	62	62	6	—
Part 2 Data analysis sheet of questionnaires on other firms' CSR (%)			
Question number	Option A	Option B	Option C	Option D
Q1	76	42	24	16
Q2	2	26	71	—
Q3	8	8	37	—
Q4	42	3	53	—
Q5	10	70	19	—
Q6	—	—	—	—
Q7	—	—	—	—
Q8	—	—	—	—
Q9	—	—	—	—
Q10	—	—	—	—
Q11	76	85	85	63
Q12	79	61	66	69
Q13	55	3	90	52
Q14	92	2	6	—
Q15	40	58	2	—

Note: "—" means no relevant data to compare.

Based on Table 4 – 3, we can get the following conclusions: for Q1, for commercial banks, the percentage is 16%, obviously lower than 76% for other corporations, which may suggest that commercial banks know about CSR less than the national level of the average; for Q13, the former is 53%, while the latter is 90%, which may suggest that on the issue that taking CSR can improve firms' long – term interests, commercial banks also know less than other corporations.

Table 4 – 4　Descriptive statistics of CSR questionnaire of commercial banks and other firms

	A	B	CC	AA	BB	CC01
Mean	0. 300000	0. 274000	0. 356200	0. 276000	0. 298000	0. 408000
Median	0. 300000	0. 300000	0. 400000	0. 100000	0. 260000	0. 370000
Maximum	0. 480000	0. 470000	0. 780000	0. 760000	0. 700000	0. 710000
Minimum	0. 100000	0. 100000	0. 001000	0. 020000	0. 030000	0. 190000
Std. Dev.	0. 171464	0. 157575	0. 339046	0. 312218	0. 272617	0. 214056
Skewness	– 0. 045244	0. 012705	0. 046256	0. 795383	0. 512043	0. 404747
Kurtosis	1. 333819	1. 473876	1. 456599	2. 040157	1. 909846	1. 726165
Jarque – Bera	0. 580072	0. 485354	0. 498051	0. 719133	0. 466080	0. 474570
Probability	0. 748237	0. 784525	0. 779560	0. 697979	0. 792122	0. 788766
Sum	1. 500000	1. 370000	1. 781000	1. 380000	1. 490000	2. 040000
Sum Sq. Dev	0. 117600	0. 099320	0. 459809	0. 389920	0. 297280	0. 183280
Observation	5	5	5	5	5	5

Material resource: arranged by econometric software eviews 6. 0 by author.

Based on Table 4 – 4, from Q1 to Q5, we can get the following conclusions that: Compared with the national survey data, seeing from the mean value, in this survey, interviewees choosing A are more, while interviewees choosing CC are less, which suggests that compared with other studies, this study pays more recognition on CSR. 99 standard deviation of this study is smaller than that of other studies, which suggests that on the recognition of CSR, this study is more reliable. This comparison further explains that in terms of the recognition of SR, commercial banks fall behind other corporations in China.

Table 4 – 5   Similarity analysis of CSR questionnaires of commercial banks and other firms

Method	(A, AA)		(B, BB)		(CC, CC01)	
	Value	Probability	Value	Probability	Value	Probability
t – test	– 0. 170432	0. 8689	0. 150661	0. 884	– 0. 288875	0. 78
Satterthwaite – Welch t – test	– 0. 170432	0. 8689	0. 150661	0. 885	– 0. 288875	0. 7813
Anova F – test	0. 029047	0. 8689	0. 022699	0. 884	0. 083449	0. 78
Welch F – test	0. 029047	0. 8689	0. 022699	0. 885	0. 083449	0. 7813

Material resource: arranged by econometric software Eviews 6. 0 by author.

Based on Table 4 – 5, we can see that t – test, Satterthwaite – Welch t – test, Anova F – test, Welch F – test refuse null hypothesis: The mean value of two valuables are equal. This suggests that this study is quite different from other studies. These differences further explain that: There are 5 questions newly mentioned in this questionnaire, which exclusively belong to the scope of commercial banks' CSR; on recognizing the importance and benefit of taking CSR, commercial banks fall behind the national level.

Table 4 – 6   Descriptive statistics on the CSR recognition
of commercial banks and other firms

	A	AA	B	BB	CC	CD	D01	DD
Mean	0. 63667	0. 700000	0. 533333	0. 496667	0. 526667	0. 083333	0. 526667	0. 613333
Median	0. 780000	0. 760000	0. 670000	0. 610000	0. 510000	0. 850000	0. 510000	0. 630000
Maximum	0. 820000	0. 790000	0. 730000	0. 850000	0. 700000	0. 900000	0. 700000	0. 690000
Minimum	0. 310000	0. 550000	0. 200000	0. 030000	0. 370000	0. 660000	0. 370000	0. 520000
Std. Dev.	0. 283608	0. 130767	0. 290230	0. 421584	0. 165630	0. 126623	0. 165630	0. 086217
Skewness	– 0. 691315	– 0. 665469	– 0. 673260	– 0. 458176	0. 182990	– 0. 585102	0. 182990	– 0. 341864
Kurtosis	1. 500000	1. 500000	1. 500000	1. 500000	1. 500000	1. 500000	1. 500000	1. 500000
Jarque – Bera	0. 520209	0. 502674	0. 507890	0. 386213	0. 284565	0. 452422	0. 297993	0. 339686
Probability	0. 770971	0. 777760	0. 775735	0. 824394	0. 867376	0. 797550	0. 861527	0. 843797
Sum	1. 910000	2. 100000	1. 600000	1. 490000	1. 820000	2. 410000	1. 580000	1. 840000
Sum Sq. Dev.	0. 160867	0. 034200	0. 168467	0. 355467	0. 011267	0. 032067	0. 054867	0. 014867
Observations	3	3	3	3	3	3	3	3

Material resource: arranged by econometric software Eviews 6. 0 by author.

According to Table 4 − 6, the following conclusions can be reached: On the fourth indicator, commercial banks are 0. 526667, while the national level is 0. 613333, which suggests that commercial banks' recognition on CSR is more based on economic benefits, and lacks necessary recognition on non − economic CSR activities.

4. 3. 2　Brief summary

First, on the importance of taking CSR, 53% Chinese commercial banks admit the key role of taking CSR in maintaining long − term interests, 68% admit the key role in sustainable development, and 90% admit the key role in improving corporate image. On understanding the meaning of CSR, awareness deviation that puts economic responsibility commonly exists in commercial banks. The conclusions of this study are that: taking CSR is in line with long − term interests, and is good for improving corporate image, and achieving sustainable development; the importance of taking CSR has been accepted by more and more Chinese commercial banks, but this awareness still falls behind the national level compared with other firms.

What's more, this study further verifies that "CSR is in positive correlation with corporate sustainable development" mentioned in the theoretical review.

Second, in terms of management system, defects obviously exist in China commercial banks. This study suggests that: Only 0. 1% interviewees are impacted by the guideline of "Equator Principle", this international green credit project for commercial banks, 72% interviewees have never heard about the relevant concept; most Chinese commercial banks haven't established specialized organizations to manage CSR; only 10% interviewees admit that their banks have conducted CSR records and release CSR reports.

It can be concluded that necessary policies and information reporting system need to be established in Chinese commercial banks, thus to manage CSR relevant issues. These problems should be gradually solved through establishing commercial banks' CSR value system.

Third, in terms of CSR practices, some problems need to be noticed. For example, on protecting staff's interests, sexism and ageism still exist. On protecting interests of clients, unauthorized fees and non − transparent charges still exist. On protecting social interests, some protruding problem still exist, for example, according to the study, over a half of interviewees admit that their banks never consider environmental standards when lending; 25% admit their banks never or occasionally carry out state's macroeconomic policies or regional development policies.

It can be concluded that many practical problems exist in the CSR practices of Chinese commercial banks. These problems should be gradually solved through making relevant standards and mechanisms.

4.4　Chapter summary

Through the case study and questionnaire analysis of commercial banks' CSR, this chapter can reach the following conclusions:

The main conclusions of studying the foreign commercial banks are that: setting up commercial ethic values, initiatively promoting the construction of citizen rights, and making contributions to society have become strategic choices of well – known foreign banks like HSBC, etc. , as a result, these banks have gained good fame and economic benefits. All these foreign commercial banks have established complete CSR mechanism, for example, expanding the proportion of outside directors in board of directors and their decision – making rights, thus to form restraint mechanisms among senior managers to protect interests of all relevant parties. All these foreign commercial banks have established information reporting system, like annual CSR report, released relevant CSR practices and contributions, and thus increased the transparency of operating and decision – making and strengthening of social supervision. The ways that these foreign commercial banks practice CSR are various, but they mainly focused on protecting interests of shareholders (like transparent operation management, sustainable development management, protecting clients' interests (such as green credit), protecting interests of employees (such as staff training and education, social welfare, and respecting cultural difference), protecting interests of suppliers and business partners (such as jointly making and enforcing CSR standards), protecting community interests (such as supporting community development, housing, employment projects), protecting interests of government and society (such as supporting state macro policies, protecting environment, and supporting charitable causes) and so on. These can serve as examples or references for Chinese commercial banks to establish their CSR standards.

The main conclusions of studying present situation, problems, reason analysis of China commercial banks' CSR are that: on recognizing the meaning of CSR, the recognition deviation of "put economic responsibility first" exists among commercial banks; on recognizing the importance of taking CSR, Chinese commercial banks have increasingly come to embrace the importance of taking CSR, and feel that taking CSR is conducive to reaching long – term interests, improving corporate image and achieving sustainable development. While this recognition falls behind the national level, there still exists room for Chinese commercial banks to improve. On management system, China commercial banks lack necessary relevant policies, system arrangement, and information reporting system. On practicing CSR, some problems need to be noticed, like sexism and ageism, unauthorized fees and non – transparent charges, indifference towards green credit policies and state micro economic policies.

To sum up, through the data analysis and case study, this chapter further verifies that for commercial banks, taking CSR is good for improving corporate fame, promoting long – term interests and sustainable development. Besides, it provides an empirical support for recognizing problems existing in Chinese commercial banks, and it analyzes reasons and finds possible solutions, and more importantly, provides some useful references for Chinese commercial banks to set up their own CSR standards and mechanisms.

Chapter 5　Commercial Banks' CSR Essence, Criteria and Mechanism

In this chapter, based on definitions, theoretical reviews, researches, model analysis and case studies in previous chapters, is aimed at elaborating on the essence of and appraisal criteria for commercial banks' due CSR. Besides, this chapter lays a solid foundation for the establishment of a shared value on commercial banks' CSR, and helps fulfill CSR in a proper way.

5. 1　Commercial banks' CSR essence and concrete methods

Previous chapters have got into detail on some vital information, concerning CSR definitions, CSR theories (stakeholder theories), commercial banks' practices worldwide (case studies), Chinese commercial banks' current situation (questionnaire surveys). In this chapter, the author generally divides Chinese commercial banks' CSR into five categories: communities and the public, customers, employees (both managers and staffs), vendors and competitors, investors (titleholders, shareholders or creditors). Chinese commercial banks must act from their own realities to fully exercise shared social responsibilities as follows.

5. 1. 1　Commercial banks' responsibilities for community and the public

Commercial banks' responsibilities for community and the public can be showing concern for public health, protecting natural environment, improving labor force quality, supporting charities programs and socially useful activities, upholding national macro – economic security and social stability, boosting community economic growth and social evolution.

(1) Showing concern for public health. Commercial banks must show concern for public health issues. For example, commercial banks must take their shared responsibility in controlling and curing infectious diseases, AIDS for example. Meanwhile, commercial banks can educate staffs about disease preventive knowledge and help improve health – care programs and medical equipment through self – financing or borrowing from other banks.

(2) Protecting natural environment. It's an unshirkable duty to protect environment on which persons or things rely for existence. Commercial banks are duty – bound, by implementing green – credit policy, to put a cap on loan to projects, which ruin the environment. In addition, banks can lend money to scientific research institutions or corporations as they seek to develop environmentally friendly technologies. By doing so, the air and river pollution caused by loan – financed enterprises will be significantly reduced. Meanwhile, commercial banks can set an example to others. A case in point is the use of recyclable, degradable, reproducible and pollution – free products. This way of working will save enormous resources for society and do immense service in environmental protection.

(3) Improving labor force quality. HR, an indispensable national treasure, is also of great significance to massive corporations, including commercial banks. Commercial banks have a role to play in several parts. First, banks should provide staffs with more accesses to education and training, making staffs more employable and having a better control over advanced technologies. Second, banks can make more contribution to state personnel training plan by investing more in or lending more money to education institutions and disadvantaged students.

(4) Supporting charity programs and socially useful activities. While earning large profits, commercial banks have the responsibility to pay back society, local areas where banks locate in particular. Charity and public welfare events are diversified in forms, such as donating money and goods to help Hope Projects (the project of building Chinese schools in needed areas with sponsorship of donators) operate and to help

disaster – striken areas out of trouble, as well as encouraging staffs to join in social love – giving activities. These efforts will not only benefit society and help recipients, but also make commercial banks themselves more popular and influential.

(5) Supporting stable national macro – economy and society. It's commercial banks' social responsibility to uphold China's macro – economic policy and help make a more stable economic and social circumstance. Cases in point are Chinese real estate and share market. If commercial banks formulate loan scheme in accordance with government's real estate price regulatory policy, the skyrocketing home price in China will be effectively curbed or even much lower. The same is true of share market. If commercial banks exercise strict control over liquidity, financial turmoil will be kept at bay.

(6) Boosting local economy growth and social evolution. Commercial banks must make contribution to local areas. First, commercial banks can hire local talents to reduce local employment pressure. This practice may greatly improve the livelihood of local residents. Second, commercial banks must pay taxes according to law rather than evade taxes or defraud the revenue. Taxes payment contributed by commercial banks can be used to spur local economy as well.

5. 1. 2 Commercial banks' responsibilities for customers

Commercial banks usually work as major strongboxes for people's saving. If commercial banks lose credibility or even go bankruptcy, Chinese depositors will suffer severe losses, and the society as a whole will be in a mess. There are several responsibilities which commercial banks must take for their customers: ensuring customers' right to choose, ensuring customers' right to be safe, ensuring customers' right to be informed, and ensuring customers' right to be heard.

(1) Ensuring customers' right to choose. Customers are entitled to choose financial services on their own. While offering services, commercial banks can not force customers to purchase financial products or services. Besides, discrimination against customers must be eradicated in commercial banks.

(2) Ensuring customers' right to be safe. Commercial banks must guarantee the security and reliability of money deposit and withdrawal, personal information, transfer of money and E – bank in particular. Banks must assure customers of money security

and private information kept confidential.

(3) Ensuring customers' right to be informed. Commercial banks must inform customers of information concerning financial products, such as fees, scale of security, and how to perform a transaction. Commercial banks must elaborate on related instruction and offer detailed guidance as customers seek to make wise decisions.

(4) Ensuring customers' right to be heard. When customers are deprived of interests or deserved services, commercial banks must make it accessible for customers to make complaint and claim so that banks can make compensation, in time, for losses suffered by customers.

5. 1. 3   Commercial banks' responsibilities for staffs

Commercial banks can fulfill its social responsibilities for employees in such ways as follow, delivering more job well – beings, eradicating sexism and sexual harassment, ensuring equal employment opportunity, improving staffs' livelihood, and providing safe and pleasant working condition.

(1) Delivering more job well – beings. Commercial banks should see staffs as part of its success stories and distribute profit according to staffs' performance. There are several things bank can do to improve job welfare. For instance, banks must assure employees of occupational pension and medical insurance; banks must pay its staffs at due time and reward those who make extra contribution to banks; and banks should be open to advice from staff and provide staffs access to join in decision – making.

(2) Eradicating sexism and sexual harassment. It's commercial banks' obligation to put an end to gender discrimination by amending labor employment system or reformulating if necessary. In a bid to prevent sexual harassment from cropping up, commercial bank must strengthen moral education and training among staffs, and stipulate penalties in detail for those who violate regulations concerned.

(3) Ensuring equal employment opportunity. In the 21st century, HR management in many corporations are challenged by aging workforce and short of high – tech talents. As a response to these challenges, commercial banks must develop a workforce of wide – ranging demographics, such as race, age, and gender and so on. To this end, commercial banks should not view gender or age as one of its assessment criteria when it

comes to recruitment. For the aged staffs, banks need to help them unleash their talents. Besides, banks should be open to talents with various races and culture backgrounds as an effort to be competitive in international arena. By doing so, banks will find their HR management system and corporate culture more friendly and inclusive.

(4) Improving staffs' livelihood. Nowadays, people are suffering from mounting work related pressure. In order to stay outstanding in company, many employees end up working very hard. It turns out to be a grave task for corporation to help employees strike a balance between work life and family activities. For commercial banks, there are many measures which can be adopted to make workers feel less pressured, improve their livelihood, and motivate them to work in a more productive way. For example, commercial banks can outsource some less important tasks to temporary or part – time workers to reduce workload allocated among bank staffs. Commercial banks can also implement flextime, condensed workweek, home – based work and holiday system to spare staffs more time to spend with family members or on other social activities.

(5) Providing safe and pleasant working condition. Commercial banks have every responsibility to provide staffs with safe working place, sheltering staffs from incidents like building collapse, fire hazard, or armed robbery. In addition, commercial banks must create a pleasant working environment, which will not only help staffs maintain healthy and motivated, but also retain talent, valuable asset of bank.

5.1.4 Commercial banks' responsibilities for vendors and competitors

Commercial banks also need to take and exercise CSR for their vendors and competitors, those with small scale in particular.

(1) On vendor front. Commercial banks should forge a strategic alliance with each vendor (cash supplier for example) to share fruitful result and pursue co – prosperity and growth. In order to achieve this goal, commercial banks should surrender part of the profit to its vendor, share some techniques with cooperators, and exchange vital information with suppliers.

(2) On competitor front. Commercial banks should follow spirit of cooperation with competitors so as to achieve win – win situation. That means commercial banks should

not pursue monopolization by elbowing out of market business peers, especially emerging ones. On the contrary, commercial banks should regard competitors worldwide as friends and allies with shared fate rather than conventionally rivals depicted in zero – sum game. Therefore, commercial banks, together with their peers, must see each other as strategic partners and stakeholder. While maintaining market order together, they can open up new vista of financial sector.

5. 1. 5   Commercial banks' responsibilities for investors

Social responsibilities of commercial banks for investors can be sorted into two parts. On the one hand, commercial banks must work harder to maximize profit for investors. On the other hand, commercial banks must strictly abide by professional ethics and run business in accordance with law. Only by doing so, can the profit gain and capital security be guaranteed to the utmost extent.

（1）Maximizing profit. As we all know, making profit is vital to the survival of commercial banks. Meantime, it's a fundamental obligation for commercial banks to create a maximum profit for the investors, making wealth increment possible. Actually, a lack of enough profit or wealth appreciation will in many occasions lead to the inefficiency in shouldering social responsibilities.

（2）Running business in accordance with law and professional ethics. Commercial banks are entities, whose credibility forms the cornerstone of survival and business operation. Therefore, commercial bank must keep business going in line with professional ethics, regulations or law concerned so as to ensure a long term investment security and profit maximization. It's the observation of law and professional ethics rather than merely generous profit that helps commercial bank achieve sustainable development, strengthen core competitiveness and compete with peers in international arena.

5. 1. 6   Summary

Above all, CSR that commercial banks should take on can be sorted into five categories: communities and public, customers, employees (both managers and staffs), vendors and competitors, investors (titleholders, shareholders or creditors) . Fulfilling these responsibilities will not only be conducive to banks themselves, but also deliver benefits to the public and stakeholders as well. Because by doing so will assure investors of security of their money, which in turn will bring banks more customers and investments as well, which underpin banks' long – term prosperity and sustainable growth.

5. 2 Criteria for evaluating commercial banks' CSR performance

Based on the above definitions, literature review, survey research, model analysis, and case study, the author puts forward an unique set of criteria for evaluating commercial banks' CSR performance.

5. 2. 1 Significance of formulating evaluating criteria

Early in 1997, Social Accountability International (SAI) formulated SA800, the first set of CSR criteria, which stands the test of the third party certification body. This set of criteria was jointly established with some transnational companies and organizations based on the charter of The International Labor Organization (ILO), United Nations Convention on the Rights of the Child (UNCRC), and Universal Declaration of Human Rights and so on. These criteria was SAI's initial attempt to make people – oriented management, commercial morality, and cultural and ideological progress more specified and institutionalized. At the dawn of the 21st century, world major financial groups laid down *Equator Principles*, EPs for short, in line with of the social responsibility of International Finance Corporation (IFC) and the environmental protection standard of The World Bank. In June 2003, 41 world – renowned banks like Citibank and Algemene Bank Nederland took a lead in carrying out these principles. Among those who adopt these principles include both developing and developed world; and the total financing of projects involved in these principles contributes over 80% of that of the world total.

In China, Textile Industry Association has established a set of standards, namely CSC9000T, aiming at providing norms for social responsibility management among Chinese textile enterprises. To be more specified, CSC9000T makes corporation management in accordance with regulations, helps companies establish labor unions, and improves the hiring system of enterprises as they work to establish sound relation with employees.

In 2006, Yi Xiaozhun, the vice minister of Department of Commerce in China, suggested during the Multinational Corporations Summit that Chinese government was working on social accountability standards based on China's reality. In addition, China's Ministry of Commerce would attach great importance to "corporate social responsibility" as part of the effort to improve the mixture of foreign trade.

Various criteria on social responsibility measurement have come into being worldwide, but they can not fully reflect the realities of commercial banks. For example, SA8000 refers mainly to labor protection of textile industry; *Equator Principles* is ineffective in urging commercial banks to shoulder their due responsibility as they are targeted at environmental protection of projects financing activities. Although China's national social responsibility criteria may work to some extent, they may not be applicable to peculiar occasions. Therefore, commercial banks, as China's textile industry did, must set a unique set of criteria on social responsibility measurement based on their own industrial reality.

In addition, the ignorance of CSR of commercial banks and the lack of related measuring mechanism will prevent commercial banks from achieving sustainable growth, and consequently hinder national economic slowdown and social evolution. Hence, it's of great significance to map out criteria for commercial banks' CSR performance appraisal.

5.2.2   Criteria for commercial banks CSR performance appraisal

It's a long, hard journey to lay down criteria for CSR performance of commercial banks. To get this work down, we need both the research findings of experts and the staunch support of government, law maker, and banking industry association. The following discuss is devoted to research work and findings, which contribute to the establishment of commercial banks' CSR performance appraisal criteria.

(1) Criteria classifications. From the above definition of CSR, literature review, survey research, model analysis, case study, and connotation analysis, the author, referring to the best practice of commercial banks outside China, divides these criteria

into two categories: one is managerial system, like corporation values, governance structure, management organ, annual report, accounting and education systems; another is real work performance, like interests guarantee of local areas, the public, staffs, customers, vendor, competitor, and investor (as shown in Table 5 – 1).

Table 5 – 1   Criteria for the appraisal of CSR performance

Indicator categories	Assessment indicators	Specific items of assessment indicators	Weight	Score
Managerial system	Corporate value	1. sustainable growth as core value	0. 01	1
		2. CSR vision included in mission statement	0. 02	2
		3. CSR objective included in growth plan	0. 04	4
	Corporate governance structure	4. diversified independent directors	0. 03	3
		5. transparent decision – making and selection of board of directors	0. 01	1
		6. established committee of CSR subordinate to board of directors	0. 01	1
	Administra – tive organ	7. specialized administrative organs established for CSR	0. 03	3
		8. designated high – level manager responsible for CSR	0. 01	1
	Annual report	9. complete record of CSR	0. 01	1
		10. public annual report of CSR	0. 03	3
	Accounting system	11. social cost included, like resources depletion, land use, environment pollution, and occupational diseases	0. 02	2
		12. social returns included, quality efficiency, environmental protection, full employment, external benefits, social security	0. 02	2
	Educational system	13. established official Code of Conduct of CSR	0. 04	4
		14. engaged in activities to enhance staffs' CSR awareness	0. 01	1
		15. lecture, training, and education about CSR among staffs	0. 01	1

Continued Table

Indicator categories	Assessment indicators	Specific items of assessment indicators	Weight	Score
Real practice performance	Local areas and the public	16. employment growth rate	0. 02	2
		17. taxation performance	0. 02	2
		18. concern about public health	0. 02	2
		19. degree of contribution to local areas' projects	0. 02	2
		20. energy conservation, emission reduction, and environmental protection	0. 01	1
		21. advocator of EPs, an agreement on credit control	0. 03	3
		22. support for and implementation of national macro – economic policy	0. 02	2
		23. financer for SMEs and student loan	0. 02	2
		24. non – profit advertisements for charitable activities	0. 02	2
	Customers	25. usual survey of customer satisfaction	0. 01	1
		26. ensuring customer's right to be informed	0. 02	2
		27. ensuring customer's right to choose	0. 02	2
		28. ensuring customer's right to be safe	0. 02	2
		29. ensuring customer's right to be heard	0. 02	2
		30. constantly improving services	0. 02	2
		31. sustainable growth and green investment schemes for customers	0. 02	2
	Staff	32. Endowment and health insurance for staffs	0. 02	2
		33. ensuring due payment, minimum wages, and allowance for overtime work	0. 04	4
		34. no discrimination against age, gender, ethnicity, and religion belief	0. 01	1
		35. ensuring safe working place	0. 02	2
		36. usual survey of staffs' opinion and more staffs involved in decision – making	0. 01	1

Continued Table

Indicator categories	Assessment indicators	Specific items of assessment indicators	Weight	Score
Real practice performance	Staff	37. ensuring statutory holidays	0. 02	2
		38. labor contract signing rate	0. 03	3
		39. the number of staffs joining in labor union	0. 01	1
		40. the number of the file of sexual harassment complaint	0. 02	2
		41. rational management by objectives for staffs and transparent performance evaluation	0. 02	2
		42. provide staffs with training and improve skills	0. 02	2
	Vendors and competitors	43. honesty and trustworthiness in business running	0. 04	4
		44. following the spirit of mutual benefit and reciprocity and forging cooperative relation with vendors	0. 01	1
		45. in compliance with market rules, no monopoly and win – win with competitors	0. 01	1
	Investors	46. management mechanisms for investment risks, innovation, and sustainable growth	0. 01	1
		47. systems for supervision, inspection, and investment information notification	0. 01	1
		48. keeping business going in accordance with law and regulation to guarantee a long – term maximization of profit for investors	0. 04	4
		49. net profit growth rate	0. 01	1
		50. return on equity growth rate	0. 03	3
Total			1. 00	100

As shown above, two categories, Managerial System and Real Work Performance, include seven assessment indicators, which are composed of two to six specific items of assessment indicators. There are fifty items in total, with each scoring one to four based on each weight among all the items. Those scoring indicators are extremely vital to the appraisal of commercial banks' CSR performance, such as CSR objective included in growth plan, established official Code of Conduct of CSR, ensuring due payment, minimum wages, and allowance for overtime work, honesty and trustworthiness in business running, and keeping business going in accordance with law and regulation to guarantee a long term maximization of profit for investors. Meanwhile, those scoring three also play crucial roles, such as diversified independent directors, specialized administrative organs established for CSR, public annual report of CSR, advocator of the EPs, labor contract signing rate, increasing return on equity.

(2) Advantages of the above criteria for CSR performance appraisal. There are at least some strengths as follows: ① Originality and uniqueness. Unlike others' (as shown in Appendix 2) , this set of criteria attaches much more significance to CSR – targeted measures of managerial system, such as corporate value, strategic objectives, accounting system, and education and training. All these well demonstrate the necessity of CSR performance on system and strategy fronts. ②Comprehensiveness and Pertinence. These criteria have come into being as a mixture, drawing on strengths of IFC's financing EPs for green project; of Social Accountability 8000 targeted at guaranteeing employees rightful interests; of standards and measures adopted by such internationally renowned commercial banks as Citibank, HSBC, and Deutsche Bank. ③Feasibility and Practicability. It's very convenient and easy to mark "Yes" or "No" as to the majority of the indicators. For other indicators, like labor contract signing rate and return on equity growth rate, appraisers may acquire access to related information without many extra efforts.

(3) Disadvantages of the above criteria for CSR performance appraisal. Certainly, there is still room for further improvement. Some indicators must be more specified so as to be more practicable, such as rights to be informed, safe, heard, and choose and other indicators like public health concern. Besides, this set of criteria is some of deficient as without being put under the test of real work in a long term. Anyway, this set of criteria will be of valuable significance to the policy – making in financial corporations concerned.

5. 3   Commercial banks' CSR value construction mechanism

Through theories analysis and empirical research, especially institutional pressure theory, people know that there are two basic ways to establish a sound CSR value. They are respectively systematic pressure and strategic benefit. However, systematic arrangement is to some extent more efficient than strategic benefit in driving a business to formulate fitting CSR Criteria, whereby commercial banks could make decisions and keep business going. Because direct strategic benefit generated by CSR – based work is not immediate and easy to be identified, and CSR performance will some of be hampered by sluggishness. The author thinks raising commercial banks consciousness as a citizen and their contribution to society are a complicated task, which can only be completed by coordination among countries, governments, non – governmental organizations, and commercial banks itself. It's a long, hard work, requiring both internal and external involvement and contribution (as shown in Figure 5 – 1) .

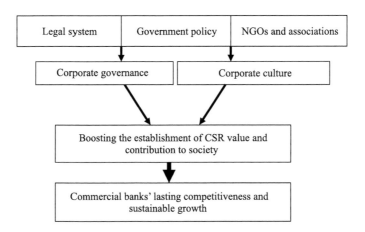

Figure 5 – 1   Project model for commercial banks' CSR value establishment

Based on Figure 5 – 1, the author argues that corporate governance and culture are internal drivers, while legal system, government policies, banking associations, and non - governmental groups serve as external drivers. It's of fundamental implication for both the internal and the external to work together to establish CSR value among commercial banks in modern society.

5. 3. 1   External contributors

(1) Compelling force of legal system. Legal system works as a key to urging enterprises like commercial banks to shoulder their due responsibilities. Most foreign companies provide clear definition of CSR based on their own reality. This is of enlightening significance, which means Chinese legislation for company must be amended in some way to put emphasis on CSR performance, legal protection for stakeholders, balance between profit and social responsibilities. Meanwhile, *Corporation Law* and *Commercial Bank Law* must make clause to determine the definition of corporation: juridical person aimed at both gaining profit and delivering benefit to society. That means while keeping a favorable balance, corporation must take into consideration such factors as employees, consumers, creditors, vendors, small and medium size competitors, local community, environmental protection, the disadvantaged, and the society as a whole. Besides, corresponding laws and regulations must be amended or enacted to guarantee the rights of stakeholders, for example, laws and regulations for fair competition, labor protection, consumers right and interest protection. Other supporting regulations like *Fair Employment Practice Law* and *Social Insurance Law* also play vital roles in regulating commercial bank CSR performance. Apart from the above, judicial departments must work harder to strengthen propaganda and education about relevant laws and regulations; and law - enforcing departments must have those commercial banks and corporations pay a heavy price for violating laws and regulations on CSR so as to cultivate society ruled by law.

All laws and regulations must be stipulated step by step. And the necessary amendment and improvement must be made to reflect the reality of CSR at different times. For example, over the past thirty years and more, *Fair Employment Practices* has been underwent amendment up to nine times. In 1972, discrimination against race, gender, age were forbidden in the amendment of *Fair Labor Law*. In 1963, equal pay for equal work was added to *Fair Wages and Salaries Act*. In 1978, protecting the rights of the pregnant was stressed in the *Pregnancy Discrimination Act*. In 1993, improving staffs' life quality and health was stated in the revised version of *Family and Medical Leave Act*. Each amendment led to a better CSR performance for staffs. China's existing law system establishment starts relatively late and is not duly amended in line with new trend of social evolution. For instance, the outdated gender discrimination still prevails in today's recruitment process among Chinese companies. Therefore, it's of valuable significance to revise relevant laws and regulations, and make improvement in CSR – related clauses so as to establish CSR value among Chinese enterprises, commercial banks included.

Based on the overall picture of China's financial laws and regulations and social credibility, China, apart from *Corporation Law* and *Commercial Bank Law*, should also speed up the perfection of laws for contract, property, guaranteed mortgage, negotiable instrument, corporate bankruptcy, financial body anti – money laundering and security. In this connection, law – makers must stipulate the basic CSR for commercial banks and make their responsibilities part of the law system. By doing so, the interests of bond – holders and other stakeholders will be well guaranteed. Besides, the bankruptcy law for financial organs must be set up to change the picture that money losses suffered by depositors after the bankruptcy are compensated by Chinese government. This adjustment, if not impossible, will lower the possibility of commercial banks' director involved in moral crisis and enhance managing staffs' social and ethical responsibility. China should also speed up the establishment of law system for social credibility, raising credibility awareness among the whole society so as to build up society of integrity and harmony. China should make adjustment to *Criminal Law*, stipulating more commercial banks criminal behaviors and preventing various financial crimes from popping out at the very first stage. A case in point is the improvement of laws and regulations fighting against money laundering. In addition, China should accelerate the establishment of laws and regulations concerning financial integrated operation and the coordinating mechanism of financial supervision. In the way, market co – manipulation by commercial bank and other financial bodies will be put to an end at a large extent; financial market and Chinese national economy as a whole will be rewarded with stable and fast growth. The last and most indispensable one is that judicial authority should strengthen law enforcement.

(2) Guiding role of government policies. Government policies play an indispensable role in helping determine the environment – related social responsibilities for commercial banks. These policies can serve to guide and spur commercial banks to voluntarily work hard to make contribution to society. There are various policy measures, including social auditing system, media public opinion, economic policies, and national strategy for social responsibilities.

1) Improvement of Social auditing system as a way to push commercial bank to put more emphasis on social responsibilities. Social audit serves as a standardized appraisal method, wide – adopted by western countries. In this connection, government departments and associations concerned have two criteria to follow when they try to appraise the performance of various corporations, like commercial banks. These two criteria are economic benefits and social benefits. The social auditing system is mainly composed of labor protection, fair employment institution, environmental protection, charitable program involvement.

2) Media propaganda to spur commercial banks to contribute more to society. Various methods, like media, Internet, and seminar, can be used to popularize the concept of social responsibilities. These methods are conducive to raising commercial banks' social responsibilities awareness and shaping a better outlook on competition and sustainable development conceived by entrepreneurs and high level managers. For example, setting new criteria for "China Economic Figures of the Year" can serve as a vital criterion to judge whether enterprises and entrepreneurs are outstanding or not. Propaganda and education can also be employed to get commercial banks' high level managers active in fulfilling CSR and making CSR part of corporation's long – term development strategy.

3) Employment of economic methods to stimulate commercial banks to shoulder more social responsibilities. In order to support social programs for public welfare and improve the livelihood of the disadvantaged group, Chinese government, apart from an increasing investment in sectors concerned based on national economy, can also resort to various economic methods to encourage commercial banks to work harder. For example, Chinese government can offer preferential policies like tax deduction and less guaranty money for deposits to those commercial banks which well perform their social responsi-

bilities in such sectors as environmental protection, poverty alleviation, and small enterprises loan. On the contrary, those which fail to fulfill their due social responsibilities must pay more taxes or huge fines.

4) Establishment of indexes for social responsibilities and sustainable development. Market should play a greater role in mobilizing public – traded commercial banks. In addition, Chinese government should map out targeted and efficient policies in a bid to popularize indexes for social responsibilities and sustainable development in financial market. In America, DJSI – Dow Jones Sustainability Index offers subjective and reliable fund investment management indexes. In Britain, FTSE Good Index Series provides CSR performance appraisal criteria. In Japan, Morningstar Japan puts forward social responsibility investment index for investment reference of those investors who attach great significance to company's integrity and sincerity. All these listed above serve as an example for Chinese government as to how to raise CSR awareness among Chinese enterprises. Based on the best practice of other countries', social responsibility and sustainable development indexes for China are expected to be shaped in line with market reality of China. These indexes will undoubtedly make Chinese enterprises, commercial bank included, focus more on how to fulfill their social responsibilities.

5) Implementation of national strategy for social responsibilities. China, based on SA8000, UN global compact and ISO26000, should formulate a set of national strategy for social responsibilities in line with its national reality. Meanwhile, China should set down supporting appraisal criteria and certification scheme as an effort to guide and spur enterprises' adoption and fulfillment of national criteria for social responsibilities performance. In this connection, Germany has a lot to offer Chinese government as almost all sectors in Germany are bounded by respective CSR criteria. Against the backdrop of existing advanced outlook on international social responsibilities, China's national strategy mainly targets at integrating various CSR criteria across China and strengthening the awareness of CSR so as to achieve standardized strategy of the performance of CSR. By doing so, Chinese enterprises will be better guided when going global and participating global competition; they will also enjoy a more smooth and faster sustainable growth as they are well adapted to new landscapes of global community and economy. As an indispensable part of national strategy for social responsibilities, national standard on CSR

must be in line with both the existing UN's convention on environmental protection, fundamental principles for human rights, core labor standards, and China's realities on the fronts of economy, politics, and social evolution. Therefore, Chinese enterprises will be able to build a society of justice, harmony, order, stable and win – win in a more regulated and efficient way.

6) Government body targeted at CSR should be set up to guarantee the efficient implementation of related strategies. A case in point is Sweden government's practice. In order to ensure a better implementation of CSR strategy, Sweden government sets up an office for partnership of global responsibilities of sustainable development. Therefore, Chinese government is suggested to set up similar CSR guiding office so as to strike a balance of policies and measures between government department and industry, as well as to organize various activities to raise the awareness of CSR among the whole society. For instance, Chinese government should hold international seminar on CSR and press conference to get government strategies well disseminated, ensure that enterprises like commercial bank fulfill their CSR while making deals in both domestic and foreign market, and also urge transnational companies to shoulder their due responsibilities constantly.

(3) Regulatory function of industry associations and NGOs. Industry associations and NGOs here mainly refer to those bodies which have an implication or act as a service provider for corporation's management. Here is a list of such bodies, domestic labor union organization, international association of multilateral social responsibilities, ILO, human rights organization, environmental protection organization, religious group, and NGO.

These associations and NGOs are major contributors in studying and formulating CSR criteria. In 2006, Chinese Federation for Corporate Social Responsibility (CFCSR for short) was set up in Beijing, the pioneer of Chinese civil NGO program. CFCSR's establishment represents the birth of the very first standardized organization of CSR in China. It will unify the whole society to conduct China's CSR programs in an organized way and offer theoretical guidance and implementation support.

The author believes that several things, listed as follow, need to be done before industry association and NGOs are truly capable of regulating commercial banks' business transaction.

1) Labor union should supervise and urge the fulfillment of CSR. China should work harder to deepen reforms in commercial banks and other financial labor union in an effort to keep competitive against the backdrop of economic globalization and market – driven economy. The main purpose of labor union reform is to make it more independent and powerful. Therefore, labor union will better perform its duties in safeguarding staffs' lawful interests and bringing the industrial relations to a new height in a coordinated and balanced way. In term of organization structure, barriers between different departments and regions must be broken before the establishment of a regional and industrial labor union, which is endowed with higher decision – making capacity. In term of organization mode, banking labor union can be set up in line with the "top – down" principle, which will generate a more democratic union, a strong body to safeguard the interests of lower level staffs. Meanwhile, labor union can exert an influence of regulation and restriction on the management of commercial banks through collectively safeguarding legal rights, whereby staffs' rights and interests are secured and industrial relation also strikes a balance. Besides, labor union should think critically and creatively, attaching more significance to staff skill training rather than merely helping staffs get out of trouble by makeshift during tough time. Under the intense employment pressure, only when employees keep skill updated, can they be well prepared to participate in today's fierce competition and make a difference on their feet.

2) Industry association should strengthen surveillance function. Financial industrial association should work hard to map out criteria for commercial banks' CSR, and urge commercial banks to join in Social Accountability International or follow the principles stipulated in *the Equator Principles* (EP). Hereafter, China's commercial banks will keep business going in accordance with SA8000, ISO9000, ISO14000, and ISO26000. Meanwhile, loan customers of commercial banks which are responsible for SAI or EP are also required to fulfill their environmental protection social responsibility by international standard in line with principles and regulation set by SAI or EP. Otherwise, these customers can never get a loan for any projects. This method will impose restriction on the delinquent conducts of both commercial banks' financing and other businesses, and customers where loan goes to.

3) NGOs are welcomed to play more influential role. Government should take its due part in setting social responsibility and allocating social welfare. For example, government should act as a law maker, resource allocator, supervisor and evaluator. While the implementer role should be played by NGOs. Compared with the developed world, NGOs' growth in China is relatively sluggish. The general absence of NGOs across China has given rise to a tougher path for commercial banks to be corporate citizens. Therefore, both Chinese government and commercial banks should strive to help NGOs play a bigger role and work with NGOs to build a society of fairness and welfare. As we all know, NGOs could be service providers for the vulnerable group, organizer and consultant for government and enterprise project, and advocator for society of justice and fairness. Working with governments at different levels, NGOs could provide care and service to those out of governments' reach, and urge enterprises to create a working environment free from gender discrimination and sexual harassment. For those layoff in poverty, enterprises should provide them with relief and offer them new ways of making a living.

In brief, a sound external financial climate can be guaranteed by government, industrial association and corresponding laws and regulations, which combined develops a governance structure of laws and regulations for commercial banks. However, an internal operation mechanism, corporate governance and culture, is also needed to raise awareness of CSR from inside (to be explained below) . On all fronts, government plays the most indispensable role as policy maker, law enforcer, resource allocator, performance supervisor and evaluator, and service provider.

5. 3. 2   Corporate internal operation mechanism

(1) Corporate governance. Based on success story of commercial banks outside China and China's reality, the author believes that a regulated governance structure can only be set down through separation of ownership and management, which means controlling shareholders can not take up managerial positions. Instead, the board of directors should appoint high rank manager in a market – based way. Besides, the scope of responsibility and relation should be stipulated clearly among commercial banks' various departments, like shareholders meeting, board of directors, board of supervisors, management, party committee; it's also the same case for the relation between the head of the board of director (party leader), and bank president (practical manager) . This definite separation is conducive to creating a corporate governance structure of clear power and responsibility, mutual check, and informed exchange. Here are some advice from the author.

1) Reasonable board of directors must be set up. There are several cases in point. Deutsche Bank chose two – tier board over shareholders meeting as its core of corporate governance. The two – tier board is more efficient than previous governance structure, and endowed with more power to take charge in more sectors. While making business decision, the board needs to take into account of interests of both non – stockholders and stockholders. In term of board component, the Citibank has a lot to offer, less inside directors and more outside professional independent directors with knowledge in management. When the outside directors represent the majority proportion in the board, commercial banks' business will be kept under sufficient supervision. Besides, the Nedbank sets up functional committee in the board of directors. This committee is an group of outside independent directors, which is responsible for supervising corporate major decision and investment and makes them in line with the fundamental interest of mass stockholders.

2) Definite and clear CSR strategy objective. Apart from improvement of board structure, commercial banks should also make CSR objective part of their development strategy objective. The Nedbank also sets an example on this front. As we can see, the Nedbank's objective for corporate governance is listed as follow: profit maximization for stockholders within reasonable range of risk; making sure that executive director's behaviors strictly comply with corporate shared moral outlook and code of conduct; striking a balance stockholders and other stakeholders, and creating targeted mechanism to prevent interests contradiction from happening; and also achieve a growth in all around ways, like economic benefit, social effect, and environmental protection, so as to become a better corporate citizen. There are two reasons why commercial banks need to figure out detailed CSR objective while making objective for development strategy. One is that CSR could provide clearer direction to bank management. Another is that CSR could also serve as a criterion for the performance of bank management.

3) Impelling – binding mechanism for commercial banks' managers. Apart from

material gain, this mechanism, with long term development strategy, is conducive to regulating banks' managers and staffs. By doing so, commercial banks can lower the risk of separation of ownership and management, and managers will attach more importance to CSR, rather merely economic gain.

4) Effective exterior supervising system. The board of supervisors must be set up to check commercial banks' business operation so as to prevent from abusing power. Besides, to make supervision an effective one, the board of supervisors must be independent, free of the influence of other organs of departments. Commercial banks must work to make the member status of the board of supervisors a profession and make sure that every member is qualified. Commercial banks also need to make sure that no one takes up position in both the board of directors and the board of supervisors, so that the board of directors, the board of supervisors and practical managers are separated from each other in interests. On this front, Germany banks stipulate that the board of supervisors must be constituted by election during stockholders' meeting, and this board is higher on rank than that of director. This board is usually constituted by representatives of stockholders, creditors, and staffs, like a representative meeting of corporate stakeholders, aimed to staffs' and creditors' rightful interests.

5) A completed and integrated accountability mechanism. Commercial banks must make detailed and corresponding responsibilities for each stakeholders, like manager selection body, the board of directors, managerial staffs, and the board of supervisors. Those who violate regulation of CSR must be held accountable and be punished with due severity.

6) Information disclosure system. This system can be used to disclose commercial banks' major decisions, record its CSR performance, regularly release its annual report on CSR, and keep its finance and major decision transparent. This system will keep the decisions by senior managers under the supervision of the public and whereby all stakeholders will be guaranteed of their interests.

7) In addition, the above measures should be in line with Corporation Law if they were used to set up and improve corporate governance structure. If they are forbidden by laws or regulations, the author suggests that some adjustments should be made to those laws and regulations. Only by doing so, the above measures can be put into practice.

Therefore, the establishment and improvement can not be fulfilled without support from government departments and legislative organs.

(2) Corporate culture. A strong corporate culture plays role in strengthening CSR awareness among commercial banks. Nowadays, commercial banks' corporate culture should embody their responsibility for social welfare, following a business philosophy of making contribution to society. Only by establishing proper moral integrity, code of conduct, and shared outlook on value, can commercial banks be one of spiritual pillars of society, and safeguard interests of all stakeholders. However, it is by no means for any groups to shape strong cultures, particularly in a short period; it takes both time and hard work step by step (as shown in Figure 5 – 2). The author believes that commercial banks could gradually develop a relative fine corporate moral culture through four different phases stated in the following graphic.

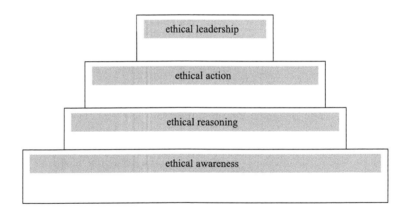

Figure 5 – 2 Model of formulation for corporate morality and culture

Note: Adapted based on Boone and Kurtz (2005).

As shown in the above model, commercial banks need to go through four phases to reinforce their corporate morality and CSR culture, and eventually figure out a wide accepted code of conduct within the whole banking industry.

The first phase is moral cognition. During this phase, enterprises can try to raise moral awareness among staffs by setting down related regulations. Based on mass opinions, commercial banks can work out a set of moral regulations or code of conduct to reflect their own realities. That means commercial banks can help their staffs differentiate right from wrong by hammering out specified code of conduct and morality, by which ethical business behaviors can be guaranteed. Meanwhile, commercial banks must explicitly stipulate their credo for CSR, informing all staffs of what CSR means in concise and detailed words. For example, one commercial bank may have its credo as follow: we firmly believe that our priority is to be responsible for all customers, and provide them with quality service; we must work hard to lower cost of business so as to ensure an affordable price for customers; we must assure our business partners of fair profit; we must be responsible for each and every staff, man and woman alike; we must be respectful of staffs' dignity and effort, and offer them safe working environment and fair salary and welfare treatment; we must help staffs assume responsibilities for family; we must offer each staff fair opportunity to secure job, gain personal growth and get promoted; we must hire responsible managers and make sure that they run business in fair and moral – accepted way; we must deliver benefits to local areas where we conduct business activities; we must strive to become better a corporate citizen, supporting charitable programs and paying taxation in time; we must be rooting for a higher standard of health care and education; we must protect environment and natural resources; we must be responsible for stockholders, generating profit for them in a rightful way; we must update our business philosophy and take measures to cope with risks of bad debts and other transactions; Only by following the above principles, can commercial banks guarantee a substantial profit for both stockholders and investors. Actually, these credos nearly cover all aspects of CSR, accurately and simply demonstrating the code of corporate conduct and laying a solid foundation for next phase of formulation of corporate morality and CSR culture.

The second phase is moral reasoning. During this phase, corporation could instill corporate culture in staffs through various trainings and education activities so as to sharpen moral judgment ability. As moral code of conduct can not provide solution to each moral hazard, commercial banks, through a series of trainings and education program, need to instill corporate spirit into each business activity, by which all staffs can make reasonable decision and offer suiting solution to moral hazards based on their ability of reasoning and judgment.

The third phase is moral action. During this phase, corporate morality and culture will be put into practice. Facing with changing situation, commercial banks need to set up hotline or advisory service division to timely cope with CSR troubles encountered by staffs and help them out of trouble. Through these measures, corporate morality and CSR culture are expected to be boosted and carried forward.

The fourth phase is moral leadership. During this phase, leaders must set themselves examples to others. Commercial banks' senior level leaders or managerial staffs need to earnestly practise what they advocate, and mobilize employees with real practice. By doing so, leaders will become more influential and charismatic among employees, which is conducive to shaping a strong corporate morality and culture. As we all know, fish begins to rot from the head. When the bank leaders behave rightly, the below staffs will do the same. Through the above four phases, a sound and strong CSR culture is expected to be formed in commercial banks.

In addition, CSR culture can also be formed through incentive mechanism and other rewarding mechanisms. For example, in order to encourage staffs to join in social activities, commercial banks can set up rewards for righteous behavior and love offering so as to commend managers and staffs who do immense service to society. With the power of role model, corporate culture becomes clearer and more solidified. Commercial banks are also suggested to give each staff two hours paid leave per week to do voluntary work in local areas. With all these efforts, staffs at all levels will gradually become active and willing to make contribution to society.

5. 4   Chapter summary

Nowadays, China is formulating a set of standardized CSR criteria; some industries are also mapping out their own CSR criteria. It's of strategic and practical significance for commercial banks to set down their own industry CSR criteria. Because the lack of CSR awareness and inefficient related appraisal system will undoubtedly hamper the growth of commercial banks, it has a bearing on China's economic security and social evolution.

In this chapter, the author, based on some definitions of CSR, theoretical review, researches and case studies of commercial banks, puts foreword some CSR performance appraisal criteria for China's commercial banks. These criteria can be classified into two categories: managerial system and real practice performance, include eleven assessment indicators, which are composed of two to eleven specific items of assessment indicators. There are fifty items in total, with each scoring one to four based on each weight among all the items.

Compared with other CSR criteria, criteria in this chapter boast originality, comprehensiveness and feasibility. This set of criteria puts more emphasis on corporate CSR self – management system, demonstrating the significance of commercial banks' CSR management on system and strategy fronts. Apart from some principles of the EPs, a international financial organization aimed at regulating investment on green project, these criteria have also learnt from some world renowned commercial banks, like Citibank, HSBC, Deutsche Bank. Although some criteria need to be more specified and be put under the test of practice, they are still of great reference value for financial decision – making departments.

Based on systematic impetus theory, we know that systematic pressure is more powerful than strategic benefit in shaping commercial bank outlook on CSR. Shaping commercial banks' CSR outlook is a complicated and systematic task, which can not be completed without supporting mechanism, internal – external coordination, perfecting law system, clear governmental guidance, supervision from industry association or NGOs, efficient corporate governance structure, and a profound corporate moral culture. Among all these factors, the author suggests that efficient corporate governance structure plays the most indispensable role in formulating corporate CSR outlook. Factors, like laws and regulations, government policy, industrial association, are actually working as corporate external governance structure. However, corporate internal governance structure and corporate culture are working as internal operating mechanisms and incentive environment, which reinforce CSR awareness and urge staffs to make more contribution to society.

Although commercial banks' managerial staffs can fulfill their CSR by improving the internal governance structure and moral code of conduct, the external supervisions from laws, government, NGOs, social media, industry association are crucial in urging managerial staffs to shoulder their due responsibility. In some cases, the external supervisions value more than the internal governance structure.

Above all, commercial banks can determine their CSR definition, appraisal criteria, and outlook on corporate culture in line with both internal governance structures and external regulations. So long as commercial banks put their CSR objectives into practice, and voluntarily conduct more activities to deliver social benefits, commercial banks' will gain higher reputation and project a better public image. A higher reputation will endow commercial banks with favorable business climate, giving rise to rising stock price in the short term and laying solid foundation for sustainable development in the long – term.

Chapter 6   Conclusions and Suggestions

6. 1   Conclusions

In this book, the author elaborates on CSR theories worldwide, Chinese commercial banks' CSR questionnaires, the CSR case studies of outstanding banks like Citibank, and systematic impetus theory— "the basic theory of the CSR formulation: system arrangement values more than strategic consideration". Based on the above efforts, the author discusses the new understanding of CSR, demonstrates the relationship between CSR and sustainable development, clarifies China's commercial banks CSR essence, and designs a set of criteria on CSR performance and mechanisms for building commercial banks' CSR outlook.

6. 1. 1   CSR boosts corporate long – term interest and sustainable development

From the surface, CSR fulfillment effectively guarantees the interests of all stakeholders. But deep down, it serves to generate long – term interests for corporations. So far, CSR study has evolved from a pure classic economic view to modern social economic view. In current market economy, commercial corporations, as an integral part of society with characteristics of a corporate citizen, should take the unavoidable responsibilities and obligations for stakeholders. In another word, they shouldn't merely focus on optimizing investors' economic interests and refuse to shoulder CSR with the excuse that taking CSR will increase corporations' operation cost and reduce profits. As we all know, corporations and society are mutually beneficial. When a corporation is making profits and being responsible for its stakeholders, it's should also actively take the responsibilities for employees, consumers, suppliers, local areas and environment protection. That means that corporations must keep business complying with regulations and commercial ethics, guaranteeing production safety and workers' health, protecting laborers' legal rights, protecting environment and natural resources, supporting charitable programs, protecting the disadvantaged group. By doing so, corporations can also shape a sound public image and increase revenues and profits as well. CSR usually includes financial aspect, legal aspect, ethical aspect, and voluntary aspect. Corporations shouldn't default each aspect for the reason of limited financial power. Instead, corporations should consider them as an endless management process, rectify the wrong notion that one charitable donation equals all corporate social responsibilities, fulfill their social responsibilities throughout their whole operation activities, and strive to benefit all stakeholders. CSR is not only an obligation that a corporation is supposed to fulfill, but also a guarantee for its goal of long – term profit and sustainable development.

6. 1. 2 Systematic pressure plays a bigger role in urging CSR fulfillment

Systematic pressure and strategic benefit consideration are the two basic drives for CSR fulfillment. As the direct strategic benefits brought by corporate social responsibilities are not immediately seen and some negative thoughts may be bred in the process, systematic pressure may, to some degree, be more effective in helping a corporation form CSR regulations and make commercial decisions that fully reflect its CSR reality. Besides, systematic drives can be divided into internal ones and external ones. Internal systematic drive mainly comes from government, policies, regulations, media supervision mechanism, and NGOs. External systematic drive mainly comes from corporate management structure, organizational and managerial system and corporate culture. Both internal and external systematic drives exert either compulsory, directory or spurring functions in the formation or implementation of CSR. It is also crucial to reinforce law – binding systematic arrangements. Poorly designed or executed regulation system can not effectively intensify the urgency of corporations improving their social responsibility performance. Systematic pressure theory offers us a meaningful perspective to deeply understand corporations' inaction in fulfilling social responsibilities and also offers Chinese commercial banks a significant theory support to build and implement the value of CSR.

6. 1. 3   Significance of commercial banks' CSR fulfillment

First, although commercial banks, uniquely – positioned, are different from other businesses in CSR essence and criteria (as international commercial banks follow the principles of the EPs), their CSR performance will have a significant bearing on stable and sound national economy and society. For example, major illegal operational activities (blindly giving out large quantities of loans, resulting in uncontrollable multiplier effect or credit risk) of commercial banks may give birth to inflation or economic crisis. Second, commercial banks' CSR outlook and performance have a radiative effect on their customers or businesses in other fields. For instance, commercial banks may, based on green credit policy, refuse to extend loans to polluting businesses, therefore directly or indirectly hampering the healthy development of manufacturing industry or other businesses in the China. Third, today's business world has entered into a relationship era. It is the key for modern commercial banks to keeping long – term core competitiveness and achieving the goal of sustainable development through actively shouldering CSR and striving to build a harmonious relationship with employees, clients, suppliers, rivals, communities and all stakeholders. What's more, China's commercial banks are indeed plagued by some problems that need to be solved.

The case studies of Citibank and other famous foreign commercial banks have shed light on their relatively sound managerial system and CSR real performance. For example, it has become world renowned commercial banks' common strategic choice to formulate commercial moral regulations and actively push for corporate citizen positions and contribute to the society. By doing so, these banks have therefore gained good social reputation and economic benefits; these foreign commercial banks have all built perfect social responsibility system arrangements, such as the arrangement of corporate governing structure and the formation of the board of directors. They perfect the arrangements of board of directors by increasing the proportion of outside directors and their right to participate in decision making to ensure the formation of a binding mechanism that protects the interests of not only stockholders but also all stakeholders involved in the hierarchic system; They also establish transparent information reporting system, such as the annual report of CSR or corporate citizen report, announcing their performance and contribution to the outside world to increase the transparency of managerial decision making and social monitoring. They have various ways of performing CSR but mainly focus on protecting the benefits of their stockholders (transparent management, sustainable development management) their clients (green credit policy), their employees (training, education and social welfare, respect for cultural difference), their suppliers and partners (work together in making CSR standards), local areas (support for the development of local areas, housing and employment projects), government and society (support for national macro policies, environment protection and charity works).

From the current situation, problem and reason analysis of China's commercial banks CSR performance, we learn that China commercial banks are still suffering from CSR problems compared with foreign commercial banks. For example, in management mechanism, Chinese commercial banks lack CSR management strategies and mechanism, annual report of CSR; They charge clients illegally for protecting their interests; their information is not transparent; they have limited contributions to charity works. Apart from external systematic reasons like imperfect laws made by the government, the internal reason is that Chinese commercial banks lack CSR management strategies and systems; relevant governing structure and corporate cultural values are not completed. The questionnaire surveys and data analysis about Chinese commercial banks CSR in this book reflects that businesses have different emphasis on economic responsibilities. Commercial banks have a stronger recognition of the importance of CSR. They have come to realize that taking corporate social responsibilities is agreeable to the long – term interests and the realization of the goal of sustainable development. However, this recognition is still below the national level, which means China's commercial banks still need to deepen their understanding of the importance and the content of CSR. In the matter of corporate system management, China's commercial banks lack necessary policies, system arrangement, and information reporting system. For instance, not even a interviewee has ever heard or been taught the EPs, the social responsibility benchmark and concept of green loan project of the International Commercial Bank; most commercial banks still haven't established targeted CSR management mechanism, social responsibility management record, or annual social responsibility report; In social responsibility exe-cution, China's commercial banks still reel from some problems worth noting such as age and gender discrimination against employees, the random charge of clients, non – trans-parent charging, the absence of social green loan policy, the ignorance of national and governmental macro – economic policies. The main reasons are: imperfect relevant poli-cies, change of economic system, loopholes existent in the governing structure of com-mercial banks, drawbacks in corporate culture.

In a word, China's commercial banks, compared with foreign counterparts, are still plagued by some problems that are in urgent need to be solved. It is of great significance for China's commercial banks to perform their CSR, so is the further studying of the sys-tematic problems concerning contemporary Chinese commercial banks' CSR.

6. 1. 4 Rich essences and unique criteria of CSR

Based on related theories and cases study, the author draws a conclusion about es-sence and criteria concerning commercial banks' CSR: businesses in different fields should have their own essence and special criteria. Commercial banks as unique com-mercial entities are no exception; they also need to set their own essence and criteria of CSR.

The essence of social responsibilities commercial banks should take is very rich and can be divided into five categories: responsibilities for local areas and the public, for clients, for employees, for suppliers, for competitors, and for investors (creditors and debtors) . Among them, responsibility for local areas and the public means showing concern about social health issues and environment protection so as to shape good public image; responsibility for clients means to guarantee clients' right to safety, knowledge, complaint and choosing the right financial service to increase clients' satisfaction and loyalty; responsibility for employees means providing employees' welfare, their partici-pation in corporate activities and living standard so as to motivate their passion for work, improve their service and productivity; responsibility for suppliers and competitors mean promoting strategic alliance and win – win cooperation to build long – term reciprocal re-lationship; responsibility for investors means to operate legally, adhere to business ethics and the principle of being honest and faithful to make sure that the funds of investors are not damaged and investors can get the sustainable and maximized returns from their investment projects. Contemporary commercial banks must take the above – mentioned responsibilities seriously and actively make preparation for the new challenges brought about by the major development trends such as global expansion, the application of new technology, financial deregulation and human resources change.

These criteria of commercial banks CSR performance are unique and targeted. According to the conclusion of CSR based on its definition, theoretical review, the researches and surveys and case studies, this book holds that: the appraisal criteria for Chinese commercial banks should cover managerial system and real practice performance, include eleven assessment indicators, which are composed of two to eleven specific items of assessment indicators. There are fifty items in total, with each scoring one to four based on each weight among all the items. This set of criteria is relatively original and practical, different from other businesses' social responsibility criteria, including management system indicator of CSR so as to demonstrate commercial banks reinforcing the importance of social responsibility management on the level of system and strategy; it has not only absorbed some contents of the EPs aimed at regulating international financial institutions interested in green projects investment, and the basic contents of SA8000 intended to protect employees' legal rights, but also borrowed the concrete standard and practice of CSR of some internationally prominent commercial banks such as Citibank, HSBC and Deutsche Bank. Therefore this appraisal criteria is more suitable for commercial banks. Although some criteria need to be more specified and be put under the test of practice, they are still of great reference value for financial decision making departments.

6. 1. 5 Internal and external system combined serve as the key to shaping commercial banks' CSR outlook

According to systematic impetus theory, constructing commercial banks' CSR outlook is a complicated and systematic project, and it is also a mechanism that requires the interworking of both internal and external system. Though it is vital for commercial banks' management to carry out CSR by strengthening internal governing structure and cultural behavior regulations, external monitoring (regulations, government management, NGOs, media opinion, industry association) is equally or even more indispensable.

Throughout the whole process of CSR building, it is of central importance for commercial banks to build CSR by actively perfecting internal and external governing structure, or optimizing relevant system arrangements. According to model analysis, commercial banks need improving regulations to restrict, maturing government policy to guide, evolving industry association or NGOs to supervise or cooperate, and a suitable corporate governing structure to control as well as strong corporate ethics and culture to fortify. All the five interworking aspects form an organic whole and play a crucial role in building commercial banks' CSR outlook. The logic behind it is that factors, like laws and regulations, government policy, industry association, are actually corporate external governance structure. Whereas, corporate internal governance structure and corporate culture are working as internal operating mechanisms and incentive environment, which reinforce CSR awareness and urge staffs to make more contribution to society.

In a word, commercial banks can determine their CSR definition, appraisal criteria, and outlook on corporate culture in line with both internal governance structures and external regulations. So long as commercial banks put their CSR objectives into practice, and voluntarily conduct more activities to deliver social benefits, commercial banks' will gain higher reputation and project a better public image. A higher reputation will endow commercial banks with favorable business climate, pushing up stock price in a short – term and laying solid foundation for sustainable development in a long term.

6. 2   Suggestions

As concluded in this chapter, it is of great significance for commercial banks to actively build and perform CSR outlook. Building such outlook can be a complicated and systematic project, and it is also a mechanism that requires the interworking of both internal and external system. Considering that, legislative departments, government, industry association, non – government organization and commercial banks should do the following works.

6. 2. 1　Legislative department should strengthen laws and regulations

First of all, apart from *Employment Contract Law*, *Environmental Protection Law* and other laws that specify social responsibilities applicable to all businesses, legislative departments should expedite improving and perfecting *Contract Law*, *Guarantee and Collateral Law*, *Bankruptcy Law*, *Financial Institution Anti – laundering Money Law*, *Financial Institution Security Law* and other economic and financial laws. These departments should also highlight the basic social responsibilities that financial corporations should take in laws and regulations, include CSR into legalized management system to protect the interests of debtors or other stakeholders; It should also build legal system for financial institution bankruptcy and change the situation where the government, for a long time, has to pay most of the personal savings after the financial institutions go bankrupt to reduce moral risk of commercial banks' administrators and raise their sense of ethics; It also needs to perfect legal system combating money laundering, amends *Criminal Law*, increase the content of commercial banks against financial crimes and effectively prevent various kinds of financial crimes. Second of all, the department should endeavor to makes laws that can promote financial institution operation, study the legislative problem of financial monitoring and mediation mechanism, and prevent commercial banks and other financial institutions from conspiring to manipulate market so as to make sure the safe operation of financial market and the stable growth of national economy. Equally important, judicial office must intensify law enforcement.

6. 2. 2　Government should play a guiding role through various policies

Government plays an indispensable role in building the environment of CSR for commercial banks. It can, through various effective policy measures, guide and spur commercial banks to actively perform their social responsibilities. Concrete policy measures are diverse. For example, establishing local areas inspection system: including economic benefits and social benefits into indicator system, comprehensively assessing and inspecting the performance of commercial banks; intensifying the function of media publication and opinion guidance through media, the internet, training, seminar and others forms of publicity to popularize the idea of social responsibility to raise the sense of social responsibility of commercial banks and other businesses; making the new standard of "Economic Figures of the Year" namely, making social responsibility contribution a new election standard for electing the advanced enterprise or great entrepreneur and utilizing publicity and education to motivate commercial banks senior management staff to take action, prompting commercial banks to make building social responsibility as a strategic long – term development goal; using economic means to encourage commercial banks to take the obligation of social responsibility. For example, government can map out some preferential policies, like taxation break, to encourage those commercial banks which do a great job in protecting environment, alleviating poverty and extending credit to small enterprise; while government can lay heavy tax on or fine those commercial banks which perform poorly in taking social responsibility; government can establish social responsibility index or sustainable development index, exerting the role of market mediation to mobilize listed commercial banks to take social responsibility actively; government can implement national and social responsibility strategies, and make a practical nation – wide CSR criteria based on current international criteria; government can also, by building assessment system and verification system, guide commercial banks to perform social responsibility actively.

6.2.3 Industrial association and NGOs should set targeted criteria and managerial system

Industrial association and NGOs can regulate commercial banks' business transaction with following measures. First, labor union must be given a role to play to supervise and boost commercial banks operation so as to safeguard staffs interests. Second, industrial association also need to do its part, for example, financial association should work hard to map out CSR regulations and criteria for commercial banks, formulate relevant managerial system. Financial association also should encourage commercial banks to join in international responsibility association or follow principles stipulated in the EPs, SA8000, ISO14000, ISO26000 as well as UN Global Compact. Third, requirements for green credit project should be established so as to regulate commercial banks' project financing loan, and urge borrowing enterprises to attach more importance to environmental protection.

6. 2. 4　Commercial banks should strengthen corporate governance structure and culture

（1）Improving board of directors to represent all stakeholders. Based on success story of commercial banks outside China and China's reality, the author believes that a regulated governance structure can only be set down through separation of ownership and management, which means controlling shareholders can not take up managerial positions. Instead, the board of directors should hire high rank managers in a market – based way. Besides, the scope of responsibility and interrelations should be stipulated clearly among commercial bank's various departments, like shareholders meeting, board of directors, board of supervisors, management, party committee; it's also true of the relation between the head of the board of director（party leader）, and bank president（practical manager）. This definite separation is conducive to creating a corporate governance structure of clear power and responsibility, mutual check, and informed exchange. Here are some advice from the author. As to reasonable structure of board of directors, Deutsche Bank chose Two – tier Board structure over shareholders meeting as its core of corporate governance. The Two – tier Board structure is more efficient than previous governance structure as the executive board is authorized to focus on a wider range of stakeholders. While making business decision, the executive board will take into account of interests of both non – stockholders and stockholders. In term of board component, the Citibank has a lot to offer, less inside directors and more outside professional independent directors with knowledge in management. When the outside directors represent the majority proportion in the board, commercial banks' business will be kept under sufficient supervision. This committee should better be a group of outside independent directors, which is responsible for supervising corporate major decisions and investment, which must be in line with the fundamental interest of mass stockholders.

（2）CSR strategy objective involved in strategy management. Apart from improvement of board structure, commercial banks should also make CSR objective part of their development strategy objective to ensure profit maximization for stockholders within reasonable range of risk; make sure that executive director's behaviors strictly comply with corporate shared moral outlook and code of conduct; strike a balance stockholders and other stakeholders, and create targeted mechanism to prevent interests contradiction from happening; and also achieve a growth in all around ways, like economic benefit, social effect, and environmental protection, so as to become a better corporate citizen. There are two reasons why commercial banks need to figure out detailed CSR objective while making objective for development strategy. One is that CSR could provide clearer direction to bank management. Another is that CSR could also serve as an evaluator for the performance of bank management.

(3) Effective exterior supervising system. The board of supervisors must be set up to check commercial banks' business operation so as to prevent the abuse of power from happening. Besides, to make supervision an effective one, the board of supervisors must be independent, free of the influence of other organs of departments. Commercial banks must work to make the member status of the board of supervisors a profession and make sure that every member is qualified. Commercial banks also need to make sure that no one takes up position in both the board of directors and the board of supervisors, so that the board of directors, the board of supervisors and practical managers are separated from each other in interests. On this front, Germany banks stipulate that the board of supervisors must be constituted by election during stockholders' meeting, and this board is higher on rank than that of director. This board is usually constituted by representatives of stockholders, creditors, and staffs, like a representative meeting of corporate stakeholders, aimed to staffs' and creditors' rightful interests.

(4) A completed and integrated accountability mechanism should be set up. Commercial banks should set up targeted CSR management supervision and regulation department so as to ensure the implementation of the strategic objectives for CSR. Meanwhile, commercial banks should perfect accountability system with corresponding responsibilities for each stakeholders, like manager selection body, the board of directors, managerial staffs, and the board of supervisors. Those who violate regulation of CSR must be held accountable and be punished with due severity.

(5) Establishment of CSR information disclosure system or annual report system.

Commercial banks should establish information disclosure system for CSR. To this end, commercial banks are supposed to make a complete record of CSR performance and regularly release annual report on CSR performance. This system can also serve as information channel to ensure a transparent financial position and other major decisions. This system makes senior managers' every decision under the supervision of stakeholders, whose due interests will be guaranteed in this way.

(6) Cultivation of strong CSR culture. A strong corporate culture plays role in strengthening CSR awareness among commercial banks. At present, commercial banks corporate culture should embody its responsibility for social welfare, following a business philosophy of making contribution to society. Only by establishing proper moral integrity, code of conduct, and shared outlook on value, can commercial banks be one of spiritual pillars of society, and safeguard interests of all stakeholders. To cultivate a strong CSR culture and provide service to society, commercial banks should formulate related code of conduct, by which staffs can well perform their duties. Commercial banks also need to get their code of conduct well understood by staffs and provide work – related training and education, based on which staffs can make precisely differentiate right from wrong, and act in line with regulation. Commercial banks also need to set up hotline or advisory service division to timely cope with CSR troubles encountered by staffs and help them out of trouble. Commercial banks' leaders must set themselves examples to others, and earnestly practise what they advocate, mobilizing employees with their real practice. As we all know, fish begins to rot from the head. When banks' leaders behave rightly, the below staffs will do the same. However, a long time stamina and diligence is needed before commercial banks' can truly set up a forceful CSR culture.

6.3 Research limitations

To sum up, issues posed in this book may be solved by conclusions drawn above. For example, the good performance of CSR can guarantee commercial banks' long – term growth and sustainable development; commercial banks have a greater role to play in fulfilling CSR than other enterprises; commercial banks should set down their own targeted CSR essence, criteria, and mechanism. There are three original ideas. The first one is about theoretical understanding. Apart from study on Confucianism's influence on contemporary CSR establishment, the author also draws on lots of CSR literatures and theories outside China. Based on these studies, the author puts forward systematic pressure theory— "systematic arrangement values more than strategic consideration in establishing CSR outlook. This theory bears great significance for both commercial banks and other enterprises to establish CSR outlook. The second one is about application. The author puts forward detailed appraisal criteria for commercial banks' CSR performance in line with China's commercial banks' CSR essence and reality, and the principles stipulated in the EP, SA8000 and "global agreement" —CSR Proposal (2000) . Meanwhile, the author also puts forward a set of systematic model or mechanism for the establishment of commercial banks' CSE outlook. These original criteria and mechanisms are conducive to commercial banks' sustainable development and other financial groups strategy deployment across China as well. The third one is about thought. As commercial banks are challenged with imperfect external and internal governance while setting up CSR outlook, government department concerned should enact complete law system and policies to regulate and guide commercial banks. Besides, NGOs should be given a role to play to help commercial banks' improve corporate governance and cultivate positive corporate culture. Although these three original ideas provide commercial banks with theoretical foundation and implementation framework to shape CSR outlook. However, due to subjective and objective reasons, there still exist some limitations as follow.

First, insufficient commercial banks' CSR literatures and documents. While studying CSR, scholars of different countries take general enterprises as study objects. There is hardly scholar doing deep research on commercial banks' CSR. Therefore, the author's opinions may not be thorough for lack of reference of related literature and documents.

Second, lack of comprehensive comparative analysis on questionnaire datum of commercial banks' CSR. Commercial banks' questionnaire has drawn on the case studies of commercial banks' CSR performance outside China, and has also been compared with datum of other enterprises across China. However, the author does not compare the empirical datum of commercial banks both in China and outside China. Besides, the questionnaire has not been tested by many comparisons in a long time. Therefore, the questionnaire quantitative analysis may not be thorough and comprehensive.

Third, commercial banks' CSR criteria and establishment mechanism without being tested by practice. As this criteria and mechanism in this book is put forward for the first time and without being applied to commercial banks' practice, defects can hardly be avoided.

6. 4　CSR challenges and further research prospects

6. 4. 1　Commercial banks' development trend and CSR new challenges

Against the backdrop of globalization and economic integration, social structure is increasingly becoming more complicated. This is true of commercial banks and some multinational companies as they expand business scopes. Meanwhile, corporations are increasingly becoming more connected. Therefore, CSR essence and scope will be interpreted in a broader sense as time moves forward. These new features and development trend of this era will bring commercial banks new challenges.

(1) Ongoing globalization and new CSR challenges for commercial banks. Undoubtedly, decades since the beginning of 21st century will be a key time for China to participate in economic globalization. With WTO accession, Chinese enterprises also boasts a greater presence in global competition. Nowadays, Chinese enterprises work harder to map out and implement overseas expansion strategies to join in global competition, like Haier Group, Chery Automobile, China National Offshore Oil Corporation, Lenovo Group, they all conduct transnational businesses to achieve global presence. China's commercial banks are also increasingly becoming players at international arena. There are two strategic models for banks' internationalization: "bring in foreign – funded banks" and "Chinese banks going global". As mentioned before, foreign banks have achieved remarkable development in China, and become more influential. At the same time, Chinese commercial banks, especially four state – owned commercial banks,

have established branches and representative offices with rapid growth rate. It is esti-
mated by the end of 2008 China boasted 559 bank branches and representative offices
scattered around the Europe, America, Hong Kong, China, Macau, China, and Asian – Pacific region. This is the largest number worldwide with an overall asset more than
$140 billion and about 20,000 staffs. Industrial and Commercial Bank of China (ICBC
for short) has more than 70 overseas branches and representative offices, and about 60
affiliated financial institutions through M&A, such as ICBC (Asia) and ICBC (London), with a total asset of over $60 billion. China Construction Bank (CCB for short)
has nine overseas branches and representative offices, with a total asset of over $ 7 bil-
lion. Agricultural Bank of China (ABC for short) has six overseas branches and representatives. In addition, joint – stock commercial banks also have established overseas
branches and representatives. Bank of Communications, China International Trust & Investment Corporation Group (Citic for short), China Everbright Bank (CEB for short),
and China Merchants Bank Co. Ltd. (CMBC for short) have established respectively
six, three, three, and three overseas branches and representatives. Generally speaking,
China's commercial banks still have a long, hard journey to go before achieving high
level of global presence and competitiveness. Because these overseas branches mainly
serve Chinese communities and are unitary in business, focusing on foreign trade. However, these overseas branches have undeniably come a long way in M&A and their marc-
hing to global market is unstoppable.

It's of vital significance for corporations to actively perform their CSR before ente-
ring global market. And CSR performance review has been the threshold for accession to
global market. With a faster global expansion, China's commercial banks are faced with
more grave CSR challenges from domestic market and international market. As for international market, CSR activities will go forward with great strength and vigor, and those
who fail to fulfill CSR will lose in implementing global strategy. As for Chinese market,
commercial banks will be edged out of market if fail to fulfill CSR against the backdrop
of increasing CSR awareness. Therefore, commercial banks should map out multilevel
CSR strategy to reflect the global development trend, as well as manage business transactions and provide financial services in line with international common practices and
CSR criteria. In Chinese market, commercial banks should well perform their CSR as

they seek strategic alliances and cooperation with foreign strategic investors. Meanwhile, commercial banks also need to make clear floor – and – ceiling share for foreign stock holding and stock selling. By doing so, foreign stockholders' behaviors will not cause much damage to the interests of banks and their customers so as to truly earn Chinese customers recognition and trust, and stay competitive in domestic market. In global market, Chinese enterprises, like commercial banks, should conduct business in accordance with local laws and regulations. Besides, commercial banks should protect environment, safeguard labors' rights and interests, show respect for cultural diversity of staffs, create jobs, participate in community service, and support charitable programs. By doing so, commercial banks will greatly improve their public image and reputation, which will help deliver more profits and enhance global competitiveness. The author firmly believe that China's overseas commercial banks will achieve development, in a harmonious and reciprocal way, with countries and regions where they conduct business.

(2) New technology application and new CSR challenges for commercial banks. Nowadays, science and technology or online banking make astounding advance with constant emergence of new technologies and industries. IT has been widely applied to financial sectors, like electronic financial service delivery and office automation, which are replacing traditional labor – intensive service system; highly efficient machines and electronic settlement network provide alternatives to manual labor, like processing deposit, loan, settlement, and consultancy. For example, ATM can provide constant and quality service around clock; POS makes it more convenient for people to shop. Actually, contemporary commercial banks are on their way to be capital – intensive. Telephone bank, online bank, and electronic transaction are replacing labor – intensive banks and saving banks' clerks from simple and mechanical work. Although application of advanced technologies can help commercial banks bring down operating cost, improve service quality and effectiveness of operation, these technologies can also give rise to substantial layoffs as machines take up many manual labor and cause staffs lose their job, which will inevitably result in series of issues like structural unemployment. Besides, application of new technologies poses another challenge when commercial banks perform their CSR: potential safety hazards. For example, how can commercial banks prevent customers' information from being leaked, and how can commercial banks assure customers of capital

security. If commercial banks are not capable of providing safe and confidential service, they may fail to fulfill their CSR for customers. Anyway, new technologies widely applied to financial sector are transforming commercial banks' business scope and services, a trend earning the close attention of today's bankers. Only by following suit and fully taking advantage of electronic technologies and other advanced inventions, can China's commercial banks comply with the developing trend of financial sector in this new era and success in future's keen competition. However, one thing is worth remembering is that commercial banks must take their due CSR seriously so as to achieve sustainable development by the virtue of the most advanced technologies.

(3) Financial deregulation and new challenges for commercial banks. In the late 20th, America began the financial deregulation, which was followed by other advanced economy, like Japan, Australia, Canada, and Britain. Financial deregulation has been a defining trend worldwide. For example, in order to suit economic reality, American government cancels interest rate ceiling for deposit and transaction accounts without interests. Therefore, commercial banks have a bigger say in interest rate and assure depositors of more fair and reasonable return from interest rate. Deregulation in financial service allows depository institutions and credit unions to be responsible for some integrated services of commercial banks. While commercial banks, by holding shares of other banks, non – bank financial institutions, and enterprises, can establish Bank Holding Company, expand business scope, and involve in mixed business transaction. But at the same time, this brings problems to the risk of banking management such as the subprime mortgage crisis. As China's economic and financial reforms deepen, financial deregulation has become a defining trend. This trend will do immense service to commercial banks and bring more grave CSR challenges as well.

Financial deregulation, as to commercial banks, serves as double – edged sword, bearing both opportunities and challenges. On opportunities front, financial deregulation makes it legally possible for commercial banks to expand business scope and conduct mixed economy so as to generate more profits. On challenges front, overlapping business scope between commercial banks and non – bank financial institutions gives rise to more fierce horizontal competition, higher operation cost and risk. With further financial deregulation and more diversified financial products, customers' idle money and service demand will go to those products with higher return rate and fine service, degenerating customer loyalty. That means the higher the interest rate banks provide, the more customers they will attract; the more favorable treatment, the more customers. In addition, market – oriented adjustment of interest rate produce wiser and more rational customers. This means customers are becoming more keen on interest rates, even those loyal customers are swaying in choosing banks and interested only in material gain. In China, high quality customers are limited in number, while banks are large in number. This unbalance makes banks scramble for customers without order and become subservient to customers. For example, commercial banks sometimes have to give lavish dinners and gifts at public expense, exploit connection and secure advantages through personal influence as they seek to win favor from customers and corporation managers. This business practice is against CSR moral criteria and can not sustain a stable relationship with clients. In a word, financial deregulation and declining customer loyalty are posing unprecedented grave challenges to China's commercial banks CSR fulfillment.

In addition, as financial deregulation and mixed management go forward, commercial banks will encounter more grave CSR challenges. As for financial deregulation, commercial banks will find it easier to collude with other financial groups. For example, commercial banks and their holding security companies can plot together to seek illegal profit by stock and bond markets manipulation. As for mixed management, commercial banks are likely to become giant financial groups, like monopoly group. In order to seek huge profit, monopoly group may exert an immense influence on government policies and makes government management less efficient, putting commercial banks under a greater moral risk. Above these two cases, commercial banks may damage customers' interests and even destabilize national economy. In critical condition, it may incur financial crisis, putting country's long – term peace and order at risk.

(4) HR changes and new CSR challenges for commercial banks. HR changes are listed as follow categories:

1) The ever larger proportion of senior employees in workforce ushers in the aging society. Demographers estimate that the number of the senior in many countries will double by the year of 2025; the number of people over 60 will surpass that of children for the first time by the year of 2050. As the aging society approaches, commercial

banks will be faced with new challenges to fulfill its CSR for the senior. Inside the commercial banks, commercial banks need to take some measures to cope with aging workforce and lack of technical employees. As for aging workforce, commercial banks should pay more attention to retirement pension, social security, and medical and health insurance. As for technical employees' shortage, commercial banks should work harder to offer employees education and training to refresh knowledge structure of the senior, cultivate more highly qualified managers and technical employees. Outside the commercial banks, commercial banks should develop more financial products targeted at the senior's retirement pension, loan for life necessities, and basic lifeline banking as part of banks' effort to fulfill CSR. Basic lifeline banking provides the underprivileged people with access to clothing, food, housing and education as they are deprived of basic banking services. In order to solve the above problems, commercial banks should make reasonable and moral decisions, considering a wider range of risks and social issues.

2) Higher employee turnover. In this new era, employees, especially those youth with high academic credentials and fine quality, are frequently changing jobs, which has become a defining trend. This trend brings corporations, commercial banks include, grave challenges. In this connection, corporations can empower employees with more social responsibilities to retain talents; corporations can, through system establishment, prevent job hoppers from leaking confidential business information and taking away high quality customers; corporations can also map out "flexible plus fixed" HR strategies, like HR outsourcing and other flexible employment means so as cope with HR shortage and even crisis anytime.

However, HR outsourcing and other flexible employment means are also criticized by side effects. Trough HR outsourcing, commercial banks contract work out to other corporation with more professional workers so as to boost production efficiency and bring down HR cost. But this practice will get laid off some inside employees of commercial banks. Through other flexible employment means, commercial banks can hire more temporary and seasonal workers to improve banks' profit, but this practice will undoubtedly result in a higher unemployment rate within banks. Besides, these temporary and seasonal workers are not guaranteed of their social benefit and security.

3) Change in relation between employers and employees as more employees begin

to hold share. As shareholding system reform of commercial banks comes to its end, many banking staffs have gained double identities: banking employees and banking shareholders. This new type of employment relationship also brings commercial banks' new challenges. For example, banking managers can not afford to simply regard their relation with employees as leader – member relation so as to order employees at random. Instead, banking managers should value employees as peers with equal status. In this case, banking managers should take more social responsibilities for employees, like giving employees bigger role to play in decision making, delegating more power to low – ranking employees, and focusing more on employees' social welfare.

In a word, China's commercial banks, like other commercial banks worldwide, have to rise up to growth trends like global expansion, new technology application, financial deregulation, and HR changes. These trends serve as both growth opportunities and CSR challenges. China's commercial banks should take these trends seriously to be well prepared for opportunities and challenges.

6. 4. 2　Further research prospects

Going forward, more work will be done as follows:

First, validation and application research on commercial banks' CS criteria and mechanism. For example, to test the feasibility and operability of these criteria and mechanism, government departments, commercial banks, research institutions, and scholars should make what kind of further efforts.

Second, comparison of commercial banks' CSR criteria and mechanism between different countries or different regions. For example, through comparison, the author can find the differences when these criteria and mechanism are used Chinese commercial banks and their overseas branches, figure out their disparity, and make further improvement.

Third, research on commercial banks' criteria and mechanism popularization in other financial institutions. Whether or not these criteria and mechanism can be used by security company, trust company, and insurance company for reference? Is it feasible for non – financial sectors to adopt these criteria and mechanism?

Fourth, research on problems brought by volatile business climate on commercial banks' CSR performance.

Appendix 1　Questionnaire Survey on Commercial Banks' CSR Performance

(For internal workers of Chinese commercial banks and foreign banks)

Commercial bank type: **A.　Chinese commercial bank**
B.　Foreign bank

The purpose of doing this research is to find out commercial banks' current CSR philosophy and problems so as to offer reference for commercial banks' decision makers. Hope you could answer the following questions (some multiple choice), and thank you for cooperation!

1. Do you ever hear or be taught the following conceptions while working or attending training in your bank?

A. CSR　　　　　B. SA8000　　　　C. EPs　　　　　D. Not familiar

2. Does your bank keep record of CSR management and release annual report on CSR?

A. Often　　　　B. Occasionally　　C. Never

3. Does your bank establish the following departments?

A. CSR dept　　B. Sustainable development dept　　C. PR dept

4. While choosing loan customers of suppliers, does your bank take into consideration of their CSR performance and environmental protection awareness?

A. Yes　　　　　B. No　　　　　　C. Not sure

5. Does your bank participate in public benefit and charitable donating programs?

A. Often　　　　B. Occasionally　　C. Never

6. Do employees enjoy social security, health care insurance and overtime wages provided by your bank?

A. All employees　B. Some employees　C. No one

7. Does your bank pay employees with salary and bonus on time?

A. Often   B. Occasionally   C. Never

8. Is there gender and age discrimination in your bank?

A. Yes   B. No

9. Does your bank keep business transactions nontransparent and unreasonable?

A. Often   B. Occasionally   C. Never

10. Are your bank's business transactions in line with national or regional macro – economic policies?

A. Often   B. Occasionally   C. Never

11. Working in bank, you thinking what social responsibilities bank should take?

A. Economic responsibilities   B. Legal responsibilities

C. Moral responsibilities   D. Voluntarily charitable responsibilities

12. Which of the following items should be integrated into commercial banks' CSR?

A. Paying tax honestly   B. Commercial ethics

C. Stockholders' interest   D. Programs for public good

13. What do you think CSR fulfillment can bring for commercial banks?

A. Financial burden   B. Lower cost

C. Long – term profit   D. Higher efficiency

14. Do you think there is a connection between CSR fulfillment and sustainable development in commercial banks?

A. Yes   B. No   C. Not sure

15. How important is it for commercial banks to fulfill CSR so as to establish their images?

A. Very important B. Important   C. Not at all

Appendix 2　China Corporate CSR Evaluation Index System

First class index	Weight	Second class index	Weight	Serial No.	Second class index	Weighting	Full score
Labor rights and interests (16)	0.58	Child labor (2)	0.04	1	whether use child labor	0.02	2
				2	ratio of juvenile employees	0.02	2
		Work compensation (5)	0.18	3	implement minimum salary standard	0.05	5
				4	pay salary and allowance on time	0.06	6
				5	pay overtime pay	0.02	2
				6	ratio of labor insurance	0.03	3
				7	inform wage composition	0.02	2
		Safety and sanitation (6)	0.28	8	Major accidents incidence	0.06	6
				9	employees accident death rate	0.10	10
				10	occupational diseases incidence	0.04	4
				11	drinking water and food storage facilities	0.03	3
		Working hours (3)	0.08	12	toilet sanitation in production area	0.02	2
				13	workers dormitory conditions	0.03	3
				14	longest working hours	0.03	3
				15	shortest rest hours	0.03	3
				16	longest overtime hours	0.02	2

Continued Table

First class index	Weight	Second class index	Weight	Serial No.	Second class index	Weighting	Full score
Human rights protection (12)	0. 26	Collective bargain rights (2)	0. 04	17	employees participation rate in work union	0. 02	2
				18	support in collective labor dispute	0. 02	2
		Ban compulsory labor (4)	0. 08	19	keep regular office hours	0. 02	2
				20	free to resign	0. 02	2
				21	free to refuse dangerous works	0. 03	3
				22	free to refuse cash and credentials deposit	0. 01	1
		Ban discrimination (3)	0. 06	23	employment discrimination	0. 03	3
				24	sexual harassment complaint	0. 02	2
				25	religious freedom	0. 01	1
		Labor discipline (3)	0. 08	26	open rules and regulations	0. 03	3
				27	ban corporal punishment	0. 02	2
				28	signature rate of labor contract	0. 03	3
SR management (2)	0. 03	Management system (2)	0. 03	29	complete SR record	0. 02	2
				30	release annual SR report	0. 01	1
Commercial ethics (6)	0. 11	customers rights and interests (2)	0. 04	31	product quality safety	0. 03	3
				32	corporate marketing image	0. 01	1
		Creditors rights and interests (2)	0. 02	33	Corporate credit record	0. 01	1
				34	customer impression	0. 01	1
		Public rights and interests (2)	0. 05	35	environmental protection record	0. 02	2
				36	tax – paying record	0. 03	3
Social welfare (2)	0. 02	Main public welfare activities (2)	0. 02	37	direct welfare activity	0. 01	1
				38	charitable donation	0. 10	1
Sum	1. 00		1. 00			1. 00	100

Note: Taken from *CSR Assessment and Empirical Study* by Li Liqing published on *South China Journal of Economics* in January of 2006.

Bibliography

[1] Anthony Saunders. Financial Institutions Management. The McGraw – Hill Company, Inc. , 2000.

[2] A. McWilliams, D. Siegel, Corporate Social Responsibility and Financial Performance: Correlation of Misspecification, Strategic Management Journal, 2003 (6).

[3] Barako G. D. , Brown A. M. Corporate Social Reporting and Board Representation: Evidence from the Kenyan Banking Sector. Journal of Management and Governance, 2008.

[4] Barnard C. I. The Functions of the Executive. Harvard University Press, Cambridge MA. , 1938.

[5] Barney J. Firm Resources and Sustained Competitive Advantage. Journal of Management, 1991.

[6] Bartlett C. A. , Ghoshal S. What is a Global Manager? . Harvard Business Review, September – October 1992.

[7] Bell M. Note to Foreign Investors: Before You Leap into China, Segment the Market. China Online News, August 29, 2000.

[8] Bloom P. N. Gundlach, G. T. Handbook of Marketing and Society. Sage Publication. Thousand Osks, CA, 2001.

[9] Boattight J. R. Ethics and the Conduct of Business. Prentice – Hall, Upper Saddle River, NU, 1999.

[10] Bottelier P. The Impact of WTO Membership on China's Domestic Economy. China Online's Book, 4 January 2001.

[11] Bottelier P. WTO and the Reform of China's State Banks, in Gerrit W. Gong (ed). China Economic Outlook, the Center for Strategic and International Studies, 2000.

[12] Bravo R. , Matute J. , Pina J. M. Corporate Social Responsibility as a Vehicle to Reveal the Corporate Identity: A Study Focused on the Websites of Spanish Financial Entities. Journal of Business Ethics, 2012.

[13] Bryan W. , Husted, et al. Corporate Social Responsibility in the Multinational Enterprises: Strategic and Institutional Approaches. Journal of International Business Studies, 2006.

[14] Cao Y. T. , Wang J. P. Social Responsibility of Commercial Banks. Financial Forum, 2008.

[15] Carr A. Z. Is Business Bluffing Ethical? In Rae S. B. , Wong K. L. (eds) . Beyond Integrity: A Judeo – Christian Approach. Zondervan Publishing House, Grand Rapids, MI, 1996.

[16] Carroll A. B. The Pyramid of Corporate Social Responsibility: Toward the Moral Management of Organizational Stakeholders. Business Horizons, 1991. Available from: http: //w3. uniroma1. it/moscarini/materiale%20seminario/Carroll. pdf.

[17] Carroll A. B. Corporate Social Responsibility: Evolution of Definitional Construct. Sage Journals Online, 1999. Available from: http: //bas. sagepub. com/content/38/3/268.

[18] CCTV Financial Channel: Top 50 index Stock. 06/06/2012. http: //baike. baidu. com/link? url = ugOlI4VPFZQibJRvsWt – m9rVQBGC6D623g _ F37McUEPckki HMKoEpvZhCn4PwkkDSJqc0Xnogf4zoe7o1td_ Iq, 2016 (7).

[19] Certo S. C. , Peter J. P. Strategic Management: A Focus on Process. McGraw – Hill Publishing Company, 1990.

[20] Chang Kai. Globalization and Social Responsibility. Business Week, 2004 (5).

[21] Channon D. F. Bank Strategic Management and Marketing. John Willey & Sons, 1986.

[22] Chen Liubin. China's CSR Governance and Reality. Dongyue Tribune, 2006 (1).

[23] Chen Liubin. Research Overview of CSR. Shandong Social Science, 2006 (2).

[24] Chen Quanquan. Social Responsibility and Corporate Sustainable Development. Shanghai Business, 2006 (3).

［25］ Chen Xiaojuan. On Public Companies' CSR. Journal of the Party School of Nanning City, 2006 (2).

［26］ Chen Xun, Han Yaqin. CSR Classification Model and Application. China Industrial Economics, 2005 (9).

［27］ Chow G. C. Challenges of China's Economic System for Economic Theory, in Garnaut R, Huang Y. (ed.) Growth without Miracles: Reading on the Chinese Economy in the Era of Reform. Oxford University Press, 2001.

［28］ Christmann P. Multinational Companies and the Natural Environment: Determinants of the Global Environmental Policy Standardization. Academy of Management Journal, 2004.

［29］ Chu Jinqiao. Better CSR Performance, Mechanism and Coping Strategies for Boosting Corporate Competitiveness. China Science and Technology Information, 2006 (1).

［30］ Claessens S. Banking Reform in Transition Countries. World Bank Working Paper, 1996.

［31］ Coase Ronald H. The Nature of the Firm. Economica, 1937, 11 (4) .

［32］ Cui Yage, Yuan Jinfang. Financial Enterprises' CSR and CSR Accounting. Financial Accounting, 2005 (9).

［33］ Dai Guoqiang. Commercial Banks' Management Science. Beijing: Higher Education Press, 1999.

［34］ Dave Hall, Rob James, Carlo Raffo. Business Studies, Causeway Press Limited, PO Box 13, Ormskirk, Lancs.

［35］ David A Waldman, et al. Cultural and Leadership Predicators of Corporate Social Responsibility Values of Top Management: a GLOBE Study of 15 Countries, Journal of International Business Studies, 2006.

［36］ David W. Gravens. Strategic Marketing. The McGraw – Hill Company, Inc. , 1997.

［37］ Davis S. Managing Change in the Excellent Banks. London: Macmillan, 1989.

［38］ Day G. S, Fahey L. Putting Strategy into Shareholder Value Analysis, Harvard Business Review, March – April 1990.

［39］ De George R. T. The Status of Business Ethics: Past and Future. Journal of Business Ethics, 1987 (6) .

［40］ Deng Jian, etc. CSR Connotation Analysis. Market Modernization, 2005 (10).

［41］ Dermine J. European Banking in the 1990s. Blackwell Publishers, 1993.

［42］ Dornbusch, Fisher, Studds. Macroeconomics. Beijing: China Remin University Press, 2003.

［43］ Drucker P. F. Concept of Corporation, the John Day Company, New York, 1946.

［44］ Du Yanguo. Traditional Confucian Outlook on Honor and Disgrace and Its Current Value. Morals and Civilization, 2006 (6).

［45］ Duckett J. The Entrepreneurial China: Real Estate and Commerce Departments in Reform Era Tianjin. Routledge, London and New York, 1998.

［46］ Dyck A. Privatisation and Corporate Governance: Principles, Evidence, and Future Challenges. The World Bank Research Observer, 2001, 16 (1) .

［47］ Dyson R. Strategic Planning: Models and Analytical Techniques. Chichester: Wiley, 1990.

［48］ Ebert R. J. , Griffin R. W. Business Essentials. Beijing: China Remin University Press, 2006.

［49］ Faulkner D. , Johnson G. The Challenge of Strategic Management. Kogan Page Ltd. , London, 1992.

［50］ Feng Z. L. , Wu M. Research on the Problem of Food Firms' CSR Triggered by Food Safety Scandals. China General Accountants, 2011.

［51］ Frankental P. Corporate Social Responsibility – A PR Invention? Corporate Communication: An International Journal, 1992, 6 (1) .

［52］ Fred Davy. Strategic Management. Beijing: Economic Science Press, 2001.

［53］ Fred H. Maidment. Management. McGraw – Hill/Dushkin, Guilford, a division of McGraw – Hill Companies, 2003.

［54］ Freeman R. E. Stakeholder Theory of the Modern Corporation, in Hoffman W. M. Frederick R. E. , Schwartz M. S. (eds), Business Ethics: Readings and Cases in Corporate Morality. McGraw – Hill, Boston, MA, 2001.

［55］ Freeman R. E. Strategic Management: A Stakeholder Approach. New York: Cambridge University Press, 2010.

［56］ Friedman M. The Methodology of Positive Economics, Essays on Positive Economics ［M］. University of Chicago Press, 1953.

［57］ Friedman M. The Social Responsibility of Business Is to Increase Its Profits. The New York Times Magazine, September 13th, 1973.

［58］ Friedman M. The Social Responsibility of Business is to Increase Profits, in Rae S. B. , Wong K. L. (eds), Beyond Integrity: A Judeo – Christian Approach, Zondervan Publishing House, Grand Rapids, MI, 1996.

［59］ Gao Fang. Corporate Moral Responsibility and Social Responsibility. Philosophical Trend, 2006 (4).

［60］ Gao Shangquan. CSR and Corporate Governance Structure. China Collective Economy, 2005 (1).

［61］ Gardiesh O. , Gilbert J. L. Profit Pools: A Fresh Look at Strategy. Harvard Business Review, July – August 1999.

［62］ Garnaut R. , Huang Y. (ed), Growth Without Miracles: Reading on the Chinese Economy in the Era of Reform, Oxford University Press, 2001.

［63］ Gemert H. V. Financial Reform in China: Bridging the Gap between Plan and Market. Shaker Publishing BV, 2001.

［64］ Genus A. Flexible Strategic Management. Chapman & Hall, 1995.

［65］ Gong Zhuming, etc. Federal Republic of Germany Financial Management System and Regulation. Beijing: China Financial Publishing House, 1989.

［66］ Goold M. , Cambell A. Desperately Seeking Synergy. Harvard Business Review, September – October 1998.

［67］ Goold M. , Campbell A. Strategies and Styles. Oxford: Blackwell, 1987.

［68］ Goss A. Roberts S. G. The Impact of Corporate Social Responsibility on the Cost of Bank Loans. Journal of Banking & Finance, 2011.

［69］ Graves S. P. , Waddock S. , Kelly M. How do You Meausure Corporate Citizenship? Business Ethics, 2001, 15 (2).

［70］ Griffin J. , Mathon J. The Corporate Social Performance and Corporate Financial Performance Debate: Twenty – five Years of Incomparable Research. Business and Society, March 1997.

[71] Grundy T. Corporate Strategy and Financial Decisions. Kogan Page Ltd. , 1992.

[72] Gu Jinglei, etc. Zhejiang Enterprises' CSR Performance Current Situation, Trend and Coping Strategies. Enterprise Vitality, 2006 (3).

[73] Guo Hongling. Literary Review on the Relation Between Foreign CSR and Corporate Financial Performance. Ecological Economy, 2006 (3).

[74] Hamel G. Competition for Competence and Inter – partner Learning Within International Alliances. Strategic Management Journal, 1991 (12).

[75] Harold Demsetz. The Theory of the Firm Revisited. Journal of Law, Economics and Organization, 1988.

[76] Harold Koontz, Heinz Weihrich. Management Science. Beijing: Economic Science Press, 1998.

[77] Hartman L. P. Perspectives in Business Ethics. McGraw – Hill Higher Education, a division of McGraw – Hill Companies, 2002.

[78] Hax A. Majluf H. The Use of the Growth – share Matrix in Strategic Planning, in R. Drson edited. Strategic Planning: Models and Techniques, London: Wiley, 1990.

[79] Heffernan S. Modern Banking in Theory and Practice. John Wiley and Sons, 1996.

[80] Henderson D. The Case against Corporate Social Responsibility. Policy, 1998, 17 (2).

[81] Hinton W. The Privatization of China: The Great Reversal. Earthscan Publications Ltd. , London, 1990.

[82] Hitt M. A. Dynamic Strategic Resources: Development, Diffusion, and Integration. John Wiley and Sons, Ltd. , 1999.

[83] Houlden B. Understanding Company Strategy: An Introduction to Thinking and Acting Strategically. Blackwell Publishers, 1993.

[84] Huang Jinqiao. CSR Interpretation in Term of Law. South China Journal of Economics, 2005 (3).

[85] Huang Wenyan, etc. On Chinese Enterprises' CSR Mangement. Science of

Science and Management of Science & Technology, 2006 (6).

[86] Huang Y. Internal and External Reforms: Experiences and Lessons from China. China Online, September 2000.

[87] Jackson, Price. Privatization and Regulation: A Review of the Issues. Longman, Chapter Three, 1994.

[88] Jackson S. E. , Dutton J. E. Discerning Threats and Opportunities. Administrative Science Quarterly, 1988.

[89] Jane E. Hughes, Scott B. MacDonald. International Banking: Text and Cases, Pearson Education Asia Limited and Tsinghua University Press, 2003.

[90] Jeff Madura. International Financial Management. South – Western College Publishing, an ITP Company, 1998.

[91] Jeff Madura. Introduction to Business, South – Western College Publishing, an ITP Company, 1998.

[92] Jiang Qijun, He Wei. CSR Strategy and Private Enterprises' Sustainable Development. Business Economics and Administration, 2005 (11).

[93] Jiang Ruochen. New Trend of Enterprise' Thinking Mode: Research on Issues Concerning Corporate Stakeholder. Business Economics and Administration, 2006 (6).

[94] Jin H. , Qian Y. Public versus Private Ownership of Firms: Evidence from Rural China, in Garnaut R. , Huang Y. (ed.) Growth without Miracles: Reading on the Chinese Economy in the Era of Reform. Oxford University Press, 2001.

[95] Johnson G. , Scholes K. Exploring Corporate Strategy: Text and Cases. Prentice Hall, 1989.

[96] Johnson G. , Scholes K. Exploring Corporate Strategy. Prentice Hall Europe, 1999.

[97] Ju Fanghui, etc. CSR Fulfillment—Based on the Analysis of Customer Choice. Chinese Industrial Economics, 2005 (9).

[98] Kahal S. E. Introduction to International Business. The McGraw – Hill Companies, 1994.

[99] Kang Shusheng. Bank System Comparison and Trend Research. Beijing: China Financial Publishing House, 2005 (1).

[100] Kang Shusheng. Commercial Banks' Internal Control System: Absorption and Innovation. Beijing: China Development Press, 1999.

[101] Khanna T. , Palepu K. Restructuring Conglomerates in Emerging Markets. Harvard Business Review, July – August 1999.

[102] Knights D. Morgan G. The Concept of Strategy in Sociology: A Note of Dissent. Sociology, 1990: 24 (3).

[103] Knouse S. B. , et al. Curves in the High Road—A Historical Analysis of the Development American Business Codes of Ethics. Journal of Management History, 2007, 13 (1).

[104] Koch, MacDonald. Bank Management. South – Western, a division of Thomson Learning, 2003.

[105] Koltchakova N. Privatisation of Public Utilities: Theory, Empirical Evidence. Lessons, Dissertation in School of Management, University of Southampton, 2000.

[106] Konosuke Matsushita, Louis Romberg. Entrepreneurs Management Art. Beijing: Culture and Art Publishing House, 1989.

[107] Lantos G. P. The Boundaries of Strategic Corporate Social Responsibility. Journal of Consumer Marketing, 2001, 18 (7).

[108] Lardy N. R. China's Unfinished Economic Revolution. Brookings Institute Press, Washington D. C. , 1998.

[109] LaRue Tone Hosmer, The Ethics of Management, Irwin/McGraw – Hill, a division of McGraw – Hill Companies, 1996.

[110] Laura P. Hartman, Perspectives in Business Ethics, 2nd edition, McGraw – Hill Higher Education, a division of McGraw – Hill Companies, 2002.

[111] Lei Xiongwen. Economic Analysis of CSR. Enterpriser World, 2006 (3).

[112] Li Jingjuan. An Empirical Study on the Relation between Chinese Listed Commercial Banks and Financial Performance. Yunnan University, 2015 (8).

[113] Li Liqing. China's CSR Legal Deficiency. Enterprise Reform and Management, 2005 (4).

[114] Li Liqing. CSR Appraisal Theory and Empirical Study: Taking Hunan Province as an Example. South China Journal of Economics, 2006 (1).

[115] Li S. , Tang W. China's Regions, Policy, & Economy: A Study of Spatial Transformation in the Post – Reform Era. The Chinese University Press, Hong Kong, 2000.

[116] Li W. Three Values Added by Strategic Charity to the Increase of CSR Management Level in China. WTO Economic Guide, 2011.

[117] Li Yanhua, Ling Wenquan. Research on Worldwide CSR and Practice Review. Technoeconomics & Management Research, 2006 (1).

[118] Li Ye, Zhao Hongjing. Commercial Banks' CSR and Finance Performance: A Study Based on Chinese Listed Banks. Financial Economics: Theory Version, 2013 (1).

[119] Li Zhicheng, etc. New SOEs Governance Problems he Reform Discussions. Economic Survey, 2005 (5).

[120] Li Zhuquan. Economic Analysis of CSR. Journal of Hunan University of Arts and Science (Social Science Edition), 2006 (1).

[121] Lin Wenqiao. CSR: New Strength for Export. Academic Forum, 2006 (2).

[122] Linge G. China's New Spatial Economy: Heading Towards 2020. Oxford University Press, New York, 1997.

[123] Liu Cangyan. CSR and Sustainable Development. Rural Finance Research, 2004 (4).

[124] Liu Liping. CSR and Corporate Benefit. Science & Technology and Economy, 2006 (4).

[125] Liu Qingfeng. Should Enterprise Fulfill CSR? . Enterprise Vitality, 2001 (9).

[126] Liu Qingxue, etc. On the Relation Between CSR and Market Competitiveness. Business Economy, 2005 (4).

[127] Louis E. Boone, David Kurtz. Contemporary Business. Harcourt College Publishers, 6277 Harbor Drive, Orlando, FL32887 – 6777, 2002.

[128] Lu Daifu. Review on Foreign CSR. Modern Jurisprudence, 2001 (6).

[129] Luehrman T. A. Strategy as a Portfolio of Real Options, Harvard Business Review, September – October 1998.

[130] Luo Jianyan. The Analysis of the Choice of Corporate Environment Evalua-

tion Indicators Based on Social Responsibility. Group Economics Research, 2006 (5).

[131] Luo W. The Construction of a Conceptual Model for the Recognization of Strategic CSR Iniatives. Business Times, 2011.

[132] Ma Fengqi. The Impact of CSR Criteria on Chinese Enterprises and Coping Strategies. Journal of Ningbo Vocational and Technical College, 2006 (6).

[133] Ma Lan. The Development of Chinese Insurance Business CSR and Liability Insurance. Journal of Wuhan Jiaotong Polytechnic, 2005 (9).

[134] Ma Qian, etc. Commercial Banks' Performance Appraisal. China Financial Publishing House, 2005 (5).

[135] Mai Y. Research on the Relationship Between Strategic CSR and Firms' Competitiveness. Special Economic Zone, 2009.

[136] McMillan J. , Naughton B. How to Reform a Planned Economy: Lessons from China, in Garnaut R. , Huang Y. (ed.) Growth without Miracles: Reading on the Chinese Economy in the Era of Reform. Oxford University Press, 2001.

[137] McWilliams A. , Siegel D. Corporate Social Responsibility: A Theory of the Firm Perspecitive. Academy of Management Review, 2001, 26 (1) .

[138] Michael D. Boton. Management of 100 Years. Beijing: China Textile Press, 2003.

[139] Miles R. E. , Snow C. C. Organizational Strategy, Structure and Process. New York: McGraw – Hill, 1978.

[140] Miller J. L. , David D. V. Hoose. Essentials of Money, Banking, and Financial Markets, Addison – Wesley, USA, 1997.

[141] Mintzberg H. The Rise and Fall of Strategic Planning. Financial Times, Prentice Hall, 2000.

[142] Molyneux P. , Altunbas Y. , Gardener E. Efficiency in European Banking. John Wiley & Sons, 1996.

[143] M. Friedman. The Methodology of Positive Economics, Essays on Positive Economics. University of Chicago Press, 1953.

[144] Nicolai J. Foss, Routledge. The Theory of the Firm—Critical Perspectives on Business and Management. London and New York, 2000.

[145] Ning Ling. Economic and Sociological Analysis of CSR and China' CSR.

South China Journal of Economics, 2000 (6).

[146] Ohmae K. The Borderless World. Power and Strategy in the International Economy, Collins, London, 1990.

[147] Pan Lizhi, etc. Bank's Contingent Governance and Creditor's Interests Protection. Financial Theory & Practice, 2005 (11).

[148] Pan Xingjian, etc. Consideration on Corporate Stakeholders and the Financial Analysis of Social Responsibility. Shanghai Finance University Journal, 2005 (6).

[149] Pava M. L. , Krausz J. The Association Between Corporate Social Responsibility and Financial Performance: The Paradox of Social Cost. Journal of Business Ethics, Dordrecht, March 1996.

[150] Perez A. , Martinez P. , Bosque I. R. The Development of a Stakeholder—based Scale for Measuring Corporate Social Responsibility in the Banking Industry. Service Business, 2013.

[151] Peter Rodriguez, et al. Three Lenses on the Multinational Enterprises: Politics, Corruption, and Corporate Social Responsibility. Journal of International Business Studies, 2006.

[152] Peter Rose. Commercial Bank Management. McGraw – Hill, 1996.

[153] Pettigrew A. M. Studying Strategic Choice and Change. Organizational Studies, 1990: 1 (1).

[154] Pindyck, Rubinfeld. Microeconomics. Beijing: China Remin University Press, 2004.

[155] Porter M. Competitive Advantage: Creating and Sustaining Superior Performance. The Free Press, New York, 1985.

[156] Porter M. Competitive Strategy. The Free Press, Macmillan, New York, 1980.

[157] Porter M. The Competitive Advantage of Nations. London: Macmillan, 1990.

[158] Prior F. , Argandona A. Best Practices in Credit Accessibility and Corporate Social Responsibility in Financial Institutions. Journal of Business Ethics, 2009.

[159] Pérez A. , Bosque I. R. The Role of CSR in the Corporate Identity of Banking Service Providers. Journal of Business Ethics, 2012.

[160] Qu Xiaohua. Research on the Relation Between Better CSR Performance and Corporate Healthy Behavior. Management Modernization, 2003 (5).

[161] Ruggiero R. (Former DG) China and the World Trading System, WTO News: 1995 – 99 Speeches, World Trade Organization, Gevena 21, Switzerland, 21 April 1997 at Beijing University, 1997.

[162] Sashs J. , Woo W. T. Structural Factors in China's Economic Reform, in Garnaut R. , Huang Y. (ed.), Growth without Miracles: Reading on the Chinese Economy in the Era of Reform, Oxford University Press, 2001.

[163] Schoemaker P. J. H. , Amit R. The Competitive Dynamics of Capabilities: Developing Strategic Assets for Multiple Futures, in Day G. S. , Reibstein D. J. (eds), What on Dynamic Competitive Strategy New York: Wiley, 1997.

[164] Schwartz P. Scenario Planning: Managing for the Future. John Wiley and Sons, 1998.

[165] Sharif M. , Rashid K. Corporate Governance and Corporate Social Responsibility (CSR) Reporting: An Empirical Evidence from Commercial Banks (CB) of Pakistan. Quality & Quantity, 2014.

[166] Shen Dayong, Wang Huochan. Social Responsibility: China's New Challenge and Strategy Against the Backdrop of Globalization. Chief Editors: Lin Huasheng, Huang Zhilian. Research on East Asian Economy—Collected Papers of the 10th International Seminar of Chinese Economic Cooperation System. Bafang Cultural Studio, 2006 (1).

[167] Shi Jining, etc. CSR Transaction Cost Theoretical Analysis. Enterprise Reform and Management, 2005 (12).

[168] Shi Lijuan. On the Legislative Perfection for China's CSR. Legal System and Society, 2006 (1).

[169] Shi Yourong. Cost for Corporation to Fulfill Social Responsibility and Strategy for Sustainable Development. Journal of Wuhan University (Social Science Edition), 2002 (9).

[170] Simpson G. W. , Kohers T. The Link Between Corporate Social and Financial Performance: Evidence from the Banking Industry. Journal of Business Ethics, Jan. , 2002.

[171] Soana M. G. The Relationship Between Corporate Social Performance and Corporate Financial Performance on the Banking Sector. Journal Business and Ethics, 2011.

[172] Stacey R. D. Strategic Management and Organizational Dynamics. Pitman Publishing, London, 1993.

[173] Stephen P. Robbins, Mary Coulter, translated by Sun Jianmin, etc. Management Science. Beijing: China Remin University Press, 1999.

[174] Stephen P. Robbins, Mary Coulter, Management. Prentice Hall, Inc. , 2002.

[175] Stiglitz J. E. Principles of Financial Regulations: A Dynamic Portfolio Approach. The World Bank Research Observer, 2001, 16 (1) .

[176] Stiglitz. Economics. Beijing: China Remin University Press, 2000.

[177] Su Qi, etc. Corporate Governance Classic Cases. Beijing: China Machine Press, 2005.

[178] Su Qi. Chinese Family Enterprise Life Circle Based on Internal Governance and External landscape. Management World, 2004 (10).

[179] Sun Hanjian. Corporate Citizen: Balance Between Social Responsibility and Earning Target. Journal of Inner Mongolia Agricultural University (Social Science Edition), 2006 (2).

[180] Tang Jiansheng. CSR in Harmonious Consumption Environment. Social Science, 2006 (6).

[181] Tang Zuocai. On the Relation Between Corporate Economic Benefit and Social Responsibilit. Journal of Hunan Institute of Socialism, 2000 (4).

[182] Taylor F. W. The Principles of Scientific Management. Harper & Brothers Publishers, New York, NY. , 1911.

[183] The Book of Changes in Vernacular Chinese Writing Group. The Book of Changes in Vernacular Chinese. Changchun: Jilin Literature Press, 1993 (9).

[184] The Chinese Institute of Business Adminstration Business Administration Editing Group. Introduction to Enterprises Management. Beijing: Economic Science Press, 1998.

[185] Thomas S. Bateman, Scott A. Snell. Management: Building Competitive

Advantage. Irwin/McGraw – Hill Companies, 1999.

[186] Thompson J. L. Strategic Management: Awareness and Change. Third Edition, International Thomson Business Press, 1997.

[187] Thompson J. L. Strategy in Action. Chapman & Hall, 1995.

[188] Thompson, Strickland. Strategic Management: Concepts and Cases. Irwin/ McGraw – Hill, 1998.

[189] Tian Hong, Lv Youchen. Research on Japanese CSR. Contemporary Economy of Japan, 2006 (1).

[190] Tian Muyu. Research on Confucian Culture's Impact on Contemporary Corporate Culture Establishment. Market Weekly, Sept. 17th, 2005.

[191] Tomas C. D. Balancing Stakeholder Satisfaction. Healthcare Executive, 1998.

[192] Ulrich D. A New Mandate for Human Resources. Harvard Business Review, January – February 1998.

[193] University of California and Berkeley University Extension, Advanced Financial Services Management (1 – 3), China Central Radio and TV University Press, 1997 – 2.

[194] Vanessa M. Strike, et al. , Being Good while Being Bad: Social Responsibility and the International Diversification of US Firms. Journal of International Business Studies, 2006.

[195] Vaughn S. Firms Find Long – term Rewards in Doing Good. Business Ethics. Dushkin/McGraw – hill, Guilford, CT, 1999.

[196] Vishwanath T. , Kaufman D. Toward Transparency: New Approaches and their Applications to Financial Markets. The World Bank Research Observer, 2001, 16 (1).

[197] Walker J. L. Financial Reform in China. China Online News, June 13, 2000.

[198] Wang Chunxiang, Zhang Zhiqiang. Corporate Objective and Social Responsibility. Journal of Dalian University, 2006 (2).

[199] Wang Dachao, etc. Chinese CSR Current Situation and Improvement Measure. The Northern Forum, 2005 (2).

[200] Wang Jiachan. CSR Management Based on Life Cycle Theory. Business Economy, 2006 (5).

[201] Wang Jingjing, etc. Economic Analysis of CSR. Journal of Western Anhui University, 2003 (6).

[202] Wang Lianhai. The CSR Trend of International CSR Investment Enterprise and Lesson for China. Finance and Accounting for Foreign Economic Relations and Trade, 2006 (5).

[203] Wang Ling. Law and Ethics are Indispensible in Enhancing and Implementing Social Corporate Responsibility—And Review of New Company Law Article 5. Seeker, 2005 (6).

[204] Wang Maolin. Strengthening CSR Awareness Before Creating a Harmonious Society. Qiushi Journal, 2005 (23).

[205] Wang Yongli. State – owned Chinese Commercial Banks' Joint – stock System Based on Deeper Understanding and Coordinate Actions. Studies of International Finance, 2005 (12).

[206] Wang Yuhua, Gao Guiping. SA8000 and its Impact on Chinese Enterprises. Market Modernization, 2006 (6).

[207] Wang Z. L. Food Security and Modern CSR. Shanghai Economic Research. Shanghai Economic Study, 2009.

[208] Wei Jin, Xu Dawei. On Chinese Corporation's Social Responsibility and Social Marketing. Macroscopic Advisory, 2006 (6).

[209] Wei Xin (President of Founder Group). Confucian Culture and International Corporations (Keynote Address). High Level Forum for Entrepreneurs Across Taiwan Strait (sponsored by Shandong Provinciall Government and The Economic Daily), Sept. 2nd, 2005.

[210] Wheelen T. L., Hanger J. D. Strategic Management and Business Policy. Addition – Wesley Publishing Company, 1989.

[211] Wheelen T. L., Hanger J. D. Strategic Management. Addition – Wesley Publishing Company, 1990.

[212] Whittington R. Environmental Structure and Theories of Strategic Choice. Journal of Management Studies, 1998, 25 (6).

[213] Whittington R. What is Strategy and Does it Matter? Routledge, London and New York, 1993.

[214] Wing Thye J. W. Structural Factors in the Economic Reforms of China, Eastern Europe, and the Former Soviet Union. Economic Policy, 1994.

[215] Wong R. Competition in China's Banking Industry. School of Business at the University of Hong Kong, Chinaonline, 2000.

[216] Wood D. J. Corporate Social Performance Revised. Academy of Management Review, 2000 (16).

[217] Wu W. Pioneering Economic Reform in China's Special Economic Zones. Ashgate Publishing Limited, 1999.

[218] Wu Xingxing, etc. Analysis of Relation Between CSR and Business Performance. Sci - Tech Information Development & Economy, 2006 (11).

[219] Wu Zhaoyun. Rational Outlook on CSR. Contemporary Finance & Economics, 2006 (5).

[220] Xia X. C. An Empirical Study on the Effect of Strategic CSR on the Asset of Brand. Journal of Tianjin University, 2010.

[221] Xiao Huamao. CSR Fulfillment Guaranteeing Corporate Sustainable Development. China Science and Technology Information, 2006 (1).

[222] Xu Er - ming, Zheng Ping. CSR Concept Model in International Operation. Study on Economics and Management, 2006 (6).

[223] Xu Jiangping. CSR Based on Division of Labor and Cooperation. Enterprise Vitality, 2006 (6).

[224] Xu Shengdao. Studies on Reform Problems Concerning State - owned Chinese Commercial banks. Financial Theory & Practice, 2005 (10).

[225] Xu Zhiping. Foreign Corporation's Social Responsibility. Market Modernization, 2006 (4).

[226] Xuan Y. F. , Feng L. H. The Implementation Foundation, Feature and Path of Strategic CSR. Journal of China Securities and Futures, 2011.

[227] Xuebing W. China's Banking Reform, Luncheon Address to the Asia Society Hong Kong Center, Asia Society May 22, 2000.

[228] Yan Shengyong, etc. Research on CSR Financial Analysis Indicators.

Communication of Finance and Accounting, 2005 (5).

[229] Yang Mei. Social Responsibility: Prerequisite for Corporate Going Global. China Tendering, 2006 (2).

[230] Yin Gefei, etc. Survey Report On China's CSR. WTO Report, 2005 (9).

[231] Yu Haihui, Wu Dingjun. China's CSR Imperfection Risk and Prevention. Technological Development of Enterprise, 2006 (5).

[232] Zehnder E. A Simple Way to Pay Harvard Business Review, May 2001.

[233] Zhan Huaxiu. CSR and Government Planning. Scientific Decision – Making, 2006 (2).

[234] Zhang Changlong. CSR Criteria for Financial Institution: The EPs. Study of International Finance, 2006 (6).

[235] Zhang Deliang, etc. Study of the Prerequisite and Perspective of the Relation Between CSR and Economic Effectiveness. China Economist, 2003 (1).

[236] Zhang Denan. CSR's Impact on Corporate Benefit. Journal of Liaoning Institute of Technology, 2006 (2).

[237] Zhang Hen, etc. Research on the Theoretical Foundation and Driving Mechanism of Contemporary CSR. Science Economy Society, 2005 (3).

[238] Zhang Hongbo, etc. Building Harmonious Society Based on CSR. Theory Horizon, 2006 (5).

[239] Zhang Rui. Corporate Responsibility: Chinese Enterprises' Compulsory Course. Economic Herald, 2006 (4).

[240] Zhang S. L. The Research Progress of Researches on Strategic CSR in China. Business Times, 2014.

[241] Zhang Weiying, etc. The Property Right Foundation of Vicious Competition. Economy Research, 1999 (6).

[242] Zhang Xingge, etc. Future Commercial Banks' Construction with E – Commerce Technology. Financial Theory & Practice, 2005 (11).

[243] Zhang Zheng. On Confucian Management Philosophy and Contemporary Value for Business Management. Economic Survey, 2005 (2).

[244] Zhang Zhiqiang, Wang Chunxiang. Western CSR Evolution and System. Macroeconomic Study, 2005 (9).

[245] Zhao Kai, Xia Shu'e. On the Significance of CSR – Psychological Orientation in Achieving Effectiveness of Chinese Corporate Culture. Social Psychology, 2006 (2).

[246] Zhao Xuming. Construction of Harmonious Socialist Society by Raising CSR awareness. Theoretical Discussion, 2006 (1).

[247] Zheng Caiming. CSR Establishment and Promotion. Development Research, 2006 (2).

[248] Zheng Junting. Corporate Marketing and Social Responsibility. Market Modernization, 2006 (6).

[249] Zheng Ruojuan. Western CSR Theories Research Progress—From the Perspective of Concept Development. Foreign Social Science, 2006 (2).

[250] Zheng Zhe. On the Establishment of CSR. Enterprise Vitality, 2006 (3).

[251] Zhong Dajun. Enterprises and Government Have Shared Role to Play in Shouldering Social Responsibility. Monthly Magazine for Study, 2006 (2).

[252] Zhong Xiaoshan. To Create New Advantages for Shenzhen Export Through Better CSR Performance. Practice and Theory of SEZs, 2006 (2).

[253] Zhou Sanduo, etc. Management Science—Principles and Methods. Shanghai: Fudan University Press, 2003.

[254] Zhou Xiaomei. International CSR and the Protection of Laborers' Rights in China. China Business and Market, 2006 (4).

[255] Zhou X. Chinese State – owned Banks May Gain From WTO Entry, Reuters. Indian Express Newspapers (Bombay) Ltd. , 1999.

[256] Zhou Yong. Social Responsibility: Theoretical Basis of Modern Corporate Culture Shaping. Business Economy, 2003 (11).

[257] Zhou Zhitian. Corporation's Social Responsibility to Care Employee. People's Comment, 2006 (7).

[258] Zhu W. M. Strategic Adjustment of Business Public Relations under the Condition of CSR. Journal of Shanghai Business School, 2006.

[259] Zhu Aiwu. Improving CSR Performance to Reduce International Trade Friction. Special Zone Economy, 2006 (4).

[260] Zhu Jincheng. China's CSR Current Situation and Prospect Against the

Backdrop of Globalization. China Mining University Press (Social Science Press), 2006 (3).

[261] Zhu Qianyu. Lesson from CSR in Western Countries. Science Improvement and Development, 2003 (12).

[262] Zhu Ruixue, Guo Jingfu. Research on Social Responsibility and Corporate International Competitiveness. East China Economic Management, 2004 (12).

[263] Zhu W. Z. ISO26000 and the Institutional Construction of Modern Businesses. Journal of Modern Economic Research, 2012.

[264] Zhuang Liumin. Commercial Banks' Business and Management. Beijing: China Renmin University Press, 1999.

[265] Zu Haiqin, etc. People – oriented Management Based on CSR Fulfillment. Heilongjiang Social Science, 2006 (2).

[266] Zuo W. , et al. Analysis of Food Security Management from the Perspective of ISO26000. Journal of Corporate Social Responsibility, 2010.